It's Been a Good Life!
Charles and Mary Beth Kennedy –
Missionaries to the World

Glenda Williams Goodson
Author of
Royalty Unveiled: *Women Trailblazers in Church Of God In Christ*
International Missions 1920 – 1970

HCM PUBLISHING
Lancaster, Texas

HCM PUBLISHING
Lancaster, Texas

It Has Been a Good Life! *Charles and Mary Beth Kennedy – Missionaries to the World* is Published by HCM Publishing

It Has Been a Good Life! *Charles and Mary Beth Kennedy – Missionaries to the World Printed in the United States of America. The views expressed are the author's only. For information address inquiries to HCM Publishing, 728 Sewell Drive, Lancaster, TX 75146*

Cover design by Halo Graphics

First Edition

ISBN: 978-0-9753342-7-0

This book is dedicated to

All who assisted the Kennedys in their Service to Humanity

FOREWORD

In 2014 a rare yellow hypergiant star was discovered 12,000 light years away from the Earth. It is called HR 5171. According to Olivier Chesneau, of the Observatoire de la Côte d'Azur in Nice, France the two stars are so close that they touch as they orbit one another. Only a dozen or so Yellow hypergiants are known in our galaxy and HR5171 is fascinating because it is so rare. And although the star has been millions of years in the making, the new discovery is very important to the study and understanding of our galaxy.

In the early 70s I met Charles "Chug" Kennedy and Mary Beth Kennedy. A younger minister at that time, I was very interested in the kingdom work of international missions and observed the couple's commitment to humanity. Here was a Caucasian former aeronautical engineer and MIT professor (also a former Quaker) who was introduced to a Black Pentecostal educator by their mutual Japanese American friend and completely committed to each other. But it was their commitment to pleasing God in the area of international Missions that I found fascinating.

History is more than about dates piled up upon one another and statistics. History is about people. Just as the history of HR5171 did not begin upon its discovery, the Kennedy's global reach did not begin in the writing of this book. *Veni Vidi Vici.* In the 1940s they began their orbit as medical missionaries to the indigent in Puerto Rico. In a rare decision for its day, this couple became the first official Church Of God In Christ long term missionary family (12 years) when they traveled with their two children to Liberia West Africa and re-established the Church's Wissekeh Mission in 1958 (founded by Mother Elizabeth White). In the 1960s, documents affirm their work in the former Soviet Union during the Cold War where they ministered in Russian prisons and hospitals.

In the chronicles of the Church Of God In Christ, the work of Charles and Mary Beth Kennedy are included among those who made our history happen. In *It's Been a Good Life - Charles and Mary Beth Kennedy - Missionaries to the World,* author Glenda Williams Goodson gives readers a starting point of research with her accurate account of the life of this missionary couple. Through the lens of these stalwart servants, the book clarifies, amplifies and promotes the work of international missions through both the Church Of God In Christ and their Community of Caring nonprofit organization. And it is designed for those who want to have a deeper appreciation of their Christian and Church Of God In Christ heritage.

Enjoy.

Bishop Charles E. Blake, *Presiding Bishop and Chief Apostle*
Church Of God In Christ, Inc.
Los Angeles, California
September 2015

A Word From Church Of God In Christ Global Missions

Bishop Vincent Matthews

Blessed be the memory of Father Charles Kennedy! I esteem Mother Kennedy that she is one of my most precious confidantes and advisors. My wife Sharon and I had seen Father and Mother Kennedy many times at convocation or AIM. After deciding to move full time ,and serve as missionaries to South Africa we became intentional about getting wisdom from them. Elder Kennedy talked less, but when he talked his words were always weighty. They were an enviable team. Sharon and I are a team and began to see them as a model to aspire towards.

In 2005, they informed us they were coming through for two days on their way to DRC (Democratic Republic of Congo) then Liberia. I had been pastoring for less than a year and we were very excited about these dream team saints coming and planned a special service.

They were to fly out on the only plane on Sunday Morning. We did not have a car and walked everywhere we went. However, I woke early went, to the corner and flagged down a "koombi" taxi to hire to take them to the airport. They had many huge bags with supplies for medical clinic, clothes for people and all kinds of supplies. We were in awe at how people this old could sustain such vibrant ministry! [Because of some circumstances] their entire trip was turned upside down and they never complained. Unruffled, they just said it has to be the Lord's will for them to be with us. They flowed like water! They never sweated or dismayed. They even should've blessed me out for messing things up, but they did not. They added value wherever they were.

This was a turning point in my ministry because I was unsure of myself and the fight God had put in me, but Elder Kennedy's wise, patient counsel and Bishop Nesbit's prophetic words to me on a walk home in the rain revolutionized my perspective on ministry.

They left on Wednesday, and I accompanied them to the airport and they made their plane. It is our policy to this day that all of our guests are accompanied until they reach the gate to fly out!!!!

The ministry the Lord has given to Sharon and I has been enriched by these two individuals being a vital part of our lives. Mother Kennedy's steps are slower now but I pray that God would bless her with longer life and better health as she continues to work in kingdom service through missions at home and abroad. May God bless Evangelist Glenda Goodson for including the great work of C.O.G.I.C missionary pioneers in her historical narratives to inspire others to serve or support The Great Commission of the Lord Jesus Christ!

Bishop Vincent Matthews, *International President*
Church Of God In Christ Global Missions
September 2015

Special Message

Mother Willie Mae Rivers

It is with joy that I pen these words concerning Mother Kennedy.

Upon seeing Mother Kennedy for the first time, I felt in my spirit that she was a woman of God with a special anointing. As time or years went by listening to her words of wisdom, I knew she was a woman who is dedicated and determined to serve God and minister to the souls of mankind in the foreign field.

Mother Kennedy also touched the lives of all with whom paths she crossed whether it is through the six homes her Community of Caring operates for Erie's homeless population or in the Democratic Republic of the Congo where she serves as Jurisdictional Supervisor for the Department of Women.

Her words of testimony and faithful service have truly impacted the lives of the women of the Church Of God In Christ.

As for me, I have been encouraged to be a true and faithful servant to my ministry as the General Supervisor leading this august body of women of this Grand Ole Church Of God In Christ.

My prayer is that the blessing of God will forever rest upon her rewarding her for the many years of labor in building His kingdom.

Mother Willie M. Rivers, General Supervisor
Department of Women, Church Of God In Christ, Inc.
Goose Creek, South Carolina
September 2015

"For God is not unrighteous to forget your work and labor of love, which ye have ministered to the saints, and do minister."
Hebrews 6:10

PREFACE

It is no light thing to write of greatness. Not greatness in the classic sense of one achieving better outcomes but rather that which is found in the vagueness of greatness: bowing before a child, showing kindness to someone where there is no audience or behaving with courage when there are valid reasons to fear. Elder Charles (Chug) Kennedy and his wife Mother Mary Elizabeth (Mary Beth) Kennedy are modern exemplars of 2,000 years of thought about who we are as Christians. And not enough people know about them! The two braved the early tide of disproval by some who expressed doubts about their love and relationship. But they recognized greatness in each other that would take them from dispensing food or clothing to those in need in their Erie, Pennsylvania hometown, to hearing Elder Kennedy's thoughtful sermons as he provided spiritual food and counsel at the Holy Trinity Church Of God In Christ (COGIC) when he pastored, to to giving sustenance to thousands around the world.

Elder Kennedy is gone but the amplification of their character built by hope and hurt lives on. There is a dignity and grace that emanates from Mother Kennedy as she finds ways to help those in need. It can be observed when, in her immaculate white uniform complete with white headdress, she whizzes by enroute to services during a COGIC convention to share her wisdom; holds court on Sundays while providing free community meals at Erie's Dayenu House (built for her nonprofit by benefactors who support her work); or afflicts the comfortable in an impassioned plea at the COGIC General Assembly in her desire to comfort the afflicted--the poor among us in America, Africa or Haiti. And one cannot but wonder how she does it all.

Welcome to a world where greatness is defined by sacrifice. This sacrificial love is beautiful in that the love of God transformed a couple into one of His most precious gifts. Today, what you do not see beyond her smile and personal charm is the steely resolve to continue in obedience to the call God placed upon her and her husband and entire family to assist who Jesus calls "the least of these."

They began serving the national COGIC in November 1956 when they were sent by International Supervisor Mother

Lillian Brooks Coffey as foreign missionaries to assist Mother Martha Barber at Liberia's Tugbake Mission Station. They did not stop when their seven year tour was over but traveled to over twenty countries sharing the Gospel of Jesus Christ while providing food, clothing and life necessities. For over fifty years, the work has been a love affair between God, the Kennedy's and the world.

This man and woman of valor exemplify what it means to surrender what could have been a financially comfortable life as the MIT trained Chug traded in a career as an aeronautical engineer to gain wealth in serving God and humanity.

Mother Kennedy is now the Supervisor of the Democratic Republic of the Congo. She and her husband were full time missionaries to Wissikeh beginning in 1958. The couple's faith, wit, energy and boldness (that only the Spirit can give), empowered them to perform some amazing feats. They served in stateside missions through the founding of the beautiful and spacious Community Country Day School, Community Drop in Centers and the Dayenu House. Their Community of Caring nonprofit is an organization feeding and housing Erie's homeless but also supports churches, schools, orphanages, and students in Liberia, Zambia, Cuba and around the world. Unquestionably, the Kennedy's dedication impacted the area in such a way that they were feted in a black tie dinner and crowned "Erie's First Couple." And at the kingdom promotion of Elder Kennedy, former student and the United States Liberian Ambassador gave a moving eulogy. The following story is one example of how Mother Kennedy's sharp mind still serves her: While the Associate Editor of the COGIC *Whole Truth Magazine* then Editor in Chief, Dr. David Hall, assigned me to write a story on Mother Kennedy. After preliminary research, I traveled to Erie and visited houses where the homeless are sheltered, the school they founded that celebrated 45 years of building lives in 2014, and Dayenu House. (Dayenu means *if God doesn't do anything else He's done enough.*) In the waning light as the day closed we talked about her unusual life all the while calls came in from around the world. *Peace be unto you,* was her standard greeting. In between calls she showed me some of her unique works of art. What was amazing is that at 80 plus years she remembered where she received each of the pieces: A beautiful chair carved with deer by students at a Ghanaian orphanage/school; a statute of Mother and Father Kennedy from the DR Congo; a hand carved cross with a malachite stand from the DR Congo. One gift, a pyramid presented by the Department of Women of the Congolese Church Of God In Christ, is very precious to her. The gift was given out of their deep poverty and she was overwhelmed that what they paid for the pyramid could have been used for sorely needed food. She recounted that it was made of the semiprecious metal, malachite, and shared that it is often thought that when the Bible talked about the Queen of Sheba, this sort of thing was from her treasures.

To be quite honest, as a child of the South, I was fascinated with this husband and wife I had seen at COGIC meetings. First of all, he was White and she was Black. And aside from this not being my norm, I heard of their world travels for the cause of Christ. The more I heard *of* them the more I wanted to hear *from* them. I received the opportunity in a COGIC United National Auxiliaries Convention when I happened upon them having lunch. As a mature woman I uncharacteristically gushed that I had admired them for many years and actually asked if I could join their group for lunch. In his quiet way Father Kennedy said sure while Mother Kennedy seemed amused. At every opportunity I would present myself to them and they patiently shared with me their delight in taking the gospel into the everywhere along with frustrations on not being able to do more on the foreign field. I have been tremendously blessed to talk with Father Kennedy and bask in the light of God's love through listening and learning from this exceptional couple.

For many years I have been a staunch advocate of Church Of God In Christ pioneers sharing their stories and bugging them to allow me to write about them has been a frustratingly delightful endeavor. Although I regret Father Kennedy is not on earth to share his story, when Mother Kennedy consented to allowing this book to be written I feel he would have been pleased. In the spirit of *Royalty Unveiled: Female Trailblazers in Church Of God In Christ Missionaries 1920-1970*, this book, *It's Been a Good Life! Charles and Mary Beth Kennedy – Missionaries to the World* is yet again a case study to point the reader to the great exploits accomplished through faith in God and hard work! I hope and pray that it will inspire readers, especially those who are considering serving as international missionaries, to seek zealously to impact the world in practical ways so that men can see their good works and glorify their Father in heaven.

Glenda Williams Goodson
Lancaster, Texas 2015

ACKNOWLEDGEMENTS

I am grateful for each grandchild, mission traveler, bishop, former teachers and students at Community Country Day School, who allowed me to interview them. Others completed the extensive questionnaire so that I not only gained insight but helpful information for the reader to have a greater knowledge of the work of this couple who define greatness in sacrificial service.

Children living on the international field in the Church Of God In Christ Mission work is rare (the children of Haiti pioneer Dr. Dorothy Webster Exume come to mind) and the Kennedy children are no exception. Throughout the three and a half years I have worked on this book, the late Charles Kennedy, Jr., Mary Kennedy Brown (born in Puerto Rico), Betsy Rooks, and Dr. Grace Kennedy (born in Liberia) have been kind. All have been or are currently working in service to humanity. Each of them shared wonderful stories (some amusing, some not) of what it meant to grow up as an international family. Cindy Kennedy seems more like a daughter than a daughter in law. Cindy did whatever she could do to help, from leaving a conference to take me to make copies of important documents or sharing her stories. Their grandchildren were wonderful in helping out. Jennifer Woodard, the oldest grandchild, shared her recollections freely, Sara is the caregiver for Mother Kennedy and each time I visited was very patient with both of us! Angela has the spirit of her grandmother in getting things done. It was Angie who keep the feet to the fire.

Bishop Vincent Matthews graciously took time from his extremely busy schedule to share personal stories of the couple's impact upon the life of his family.

Thank you Supervisor Romanetha Stallworth (Kentucky First) and Chaplain Marva Cromartie Nyema for your excellent fact checking and proofreading skills.

I thank God for my mother, Mother Gladys Williams who at this writing is almost 94 years old, always inspires and encourages me to continue the assignment God has given.

Pastor Robert L. Williams, First Lady Margaret Williams the entire family of The Historic Open Door Church prays for me and inspires me to do greater works for the Lord. I thank God for my Jurisdictional Prelate, Bishop James E. Hornsby and his wife, First Lady Janis Hornsby for their encouragement.

I will never forget the memory of my late husband and prophetic priest, George, who supported my every undertaking by encouraging me that "Lady, I may not live to see it, but your hard work is going to pay off." And it is, with me being a blessing to generations who will read and be inspired.

And to the woman who allowed me to further present her and her husband's story to the world I simply want to say thank you Mother Kennedy, a mighty woman of valor! I am so humbled to call you Mother and Friend.

INTRODUCTION

Most often, history is represented as tangled coils so intertwined as to make it impossible to isolate any one factor as key to past events. But the telling of the past is important to make sense of the present and create strategies for the future. Of history, Napoleon writes, "the reading of history...made me feel I was capable of achieving as much as the men who are placed in the highest of our annals." I said in my book on international missionaries: History Informs. History Misinforms. While the idea is not mine originally, I hold true to both the quote and the axiom. The writing of the history of the Church Of God In Christ by its adherents is so recent that the great life stories of many heroes and sheroes—how they sacrificed for the cause of Christ and held to their doctrinal belief in holiness, sanctification and Spirit baptism with the sign of speaking in tongues despite marginalization—have been lost. To gain insight on Charles and Mary Elizabeth

Elizabeth Kennedy's life, I teased through boxes of photos, documents and listened to personal stories. *It's Been a Good Life!* moves the reader into areas foreign to us and they will discover models to imitate. The first two chapters tell of their nativity as well as how God uniquely placed them together as *humans* whose love transcended race. Their beginnings will provide inspiration to individuals that the two, from a diversity of races, cultures, occupations and stratum of life, provide hope for others to believe that they can achieve.

The preponderance of history is about winners. Some would view their lack of "things and stuff" and conclude they are not counted in that great winner's circle called the individualistic approach leading to American achievement. And that rings true, however, as Chapters 3 and 4 point out, their eventful life is a roadmap to what it means to be a winner with balance. While never questioning the motives of individuals who did not work in the trenches of the inner city or Third World countries, they sacrificed accoutrements one would hold dear such as the prestige of the haute bourgeoisie and boldly ventured into the highways and hedges of the world to bring the light of God's love for the greater cause of Christian of service. While Rev. Charles (Chug) Kennedy is gone, the guiding principle these giants of the faith moved in, *Love Can Change the World,* lives on through Mary Elizabeth Kennedy's continued service and that of their children, grandchildren and those fortunate enough to be influenced by their highly coveted tutelage.

While visiting the Erie, Pennsylvania home of the woman we affectionately call Mother Kennedy she instructed me to bring an art object from her China cabinet. It was a figure of an ugly little man dressed in wonderful and colorful blue apparel holding a bouquet of red roses. She asked that I guess what the figure was made of. Paper Mache, of course. Calling her daughter, she gave another hint. It was made by Soviet Union prisoners and Mary correctly guessed it was made of bread. She then shared that when she and her husband visited a Russian prison during the Cold War the prisoners presented her with their handiwork. Religion was a threat to the governments of Communist countries and in fact Christianity had been appropriated by Western propagandists for their anti-communist cache. So the fact that religion mattered in Russia during the Cold War was not obvious to me and a barrage of questions followed – *why were they in Russia during the Cold War and more importantly what did they do to negotiate to visit a Russian prison?* The story that unfolded was fascinating including the fact that they lived with a Russian widow who was unable to speak English with them unable to speak Russian minus an interpreter but yet able to communicate.

Additionally, the couple ministered at a Russian hospital. At the end of our exchange she smiled and exclaimed, *"It's Been A Good Life!"*

The stories in Chapters 5 through 7 share the Kennedy's work to build a legacy for Christian obedience. They risked their health to minister in a Liberian leper colony, reprimanded a recalcitrant national in order to restore him to the fold, built a school for troubled Pennsylvania youth and labored untiringly as true yokefellows to fulfill their assignment to Christ's Great Commission. It also describes her efforts to continue after the transition of her husband providing insight into what it really means to allow God to use a life.

They are not the first missionary couple to have accepted the call to live, begin their family, educate and minister in areas foreign to them. Christian missionaries such as Charles and Mary Beth Kennedy have worked together to spread the gospel of Jesus Christ for centuries beginning with Aquila and Priscilla (1 Corinthians 16:19). Chapter 8 includes tributes from biological and spiritual offspring while the final chapter shares their creativeness and resourcefulness and some of the honors they have received as a result of their work.

The missionary work of this couple has spanned the globe since they began in Puerto Rico. My endeavor, indeed my calling, in writing this and other histories of Church Of God In Christ pioneers is to inspire ordinary people to attempt and accomplish extraordinary achievements.

Glenda Williams Goodson
Lancaster, Texas
September 2015

The Genesis

In the 1940s a White male Quaker is introduced to a Black female Pentecostal by a Japanese American mutual friend. They meet, fall in love and marry thus beginning what would become a life of love and service. Like their color which would later heighten the possibility of diversity in ministry, their early lives could not have been more different.

Charles Cunningham Kennedy was born on May 25, 1921 to Emma Weidaw Kennedy and Edward Cunningham Kennedy in Easton, Pennsylvania. His mother died when he was young and he was raised by William and Catherine Harless. From the time he was a child his life was happy — celebrating Easter playing cowboys and Indians, enjoying his tricycle, train set and others toys, digging for fish worms, and playing football with his brothers Nelson, Dave, Edward Stewart (Ted) and Ken. His love for the sea began early as the family took pleasure in days at the beach and he became a skilled seaman.

He lived his childhood and adolescence years in Long Island, New York where he was brought up in a large two story home with a porch that wrapped around the house. They were an extremely scholarly family: older brother Nelson would become a physician, and Ted earned a PhD in Mathematics finding employment in the field of the history of exact sciences in the Islamic Middle Ages (Fulbright Professor, University of Tehran, Visiting Scholar, Institute for the History of Arabic Science, University of Aleppo).

Charles too was a brilliant student and after high school graduation he was accepted into one of the most prestigious universities in America, Massachusetts Institute of Technology (MIT). From its 1846 beginnings, MIT drew students who were interested in scientific education. After graduating as an aeronautical engineer, he worked briefly as a MIT instructor. He was a member of the Sigma Chi Engineering Honor Society. He also taught at the historically Black Howard University where he was one of only a few White professors.

Charles became a Christian early in life. A self-identified pacifist, he was known as a man of peace and friend of the people, and worked with the American Friends Service Committee. (The American Friends Service Committee was formed in 1917 during World War I. At this time, it was common for young Quaker men who opposed war service to be imprisoned as traitors, although eventually society would come to recognize them as conscientious objectors. The American Friends Service Committee represented a way that Quakers and others could serve their country but also stay true to their pacifist values.}

Kennedy's heart's desire was that "the earth will be filled with the knowledge of the glory of the Lord." To that end, this member of the American Scientific Association, dedicated his life to studying the integration of theology and science. An oblate of the Benedictine Order and author of an unpublished book on intelligent design, he oftentimes shared his views with a wide audience. (See Chapter 9 for an example of Elder Kennedy's thoughtful writing.)

Rev. Thomas Grant Lee and Mary Ann Holloway Lee welcomed Mary Elizabeth Lee into their home on August 14, 1926 in New Castle, Pennsylvania. The delivery had gone well and her parents lavished love upon their new daughter as they did her brothers Tommy, Dicky and Bobby. By the time she was two years old her family relocated from New Castle to Erie, historically a part of the Iroquois Nation. Ironically, Iroquois law translates The Great Law of Peace. Chug and Mary Beth continued Chug's passion for peace throughout their lives.

Early in Mary Beth's life her parents observed several things about their daughter: she was inclined to prayer and meditation, she was a leader and she was reflective in pursuing the intellectual life. When she was only three years old, her mother told her, she prayed for people. Her mother's close friend was given to severe headaches and on a visit to Mary Beth's childhood home, the woman's pain was so severe she was forced to lie down. Mary Beth laid her hands on her and prayed. They also noted that their daughter was a leader even in her own family. Her brothers was big and athletic. Tommy was the oldest, Dicky was a boxer and Bobby was a football player and later became a pastor. Mary Beth had a penchant for the intellectual life and was a poet and writer while she was young.

Her parents, committed Christians, affiliated with the Church of God, founded as a Christian union in 1886 which later embraced the New Testament doctrine of sanctification, divine healing and Spirit Baptism that included speaking in tongues. Although its state assemblies, international assemblies and church institutions had been integrated at the local level, churches have been generally Black or White.[1] After moving to Erie her mother visited the White Church of God with the intention to join. She was informed perhaps she would be more comfortable with her own kind. It was then the family affiliated with the Church Of God In Christ.

The Church Of God In Christ was established in 1897 as a Holiness church by former Baptist ministers Charles Price Jones and Charles Harrison Mason. After journeying to Los Angeles, California and attending the Azusa Street Revival Mason was Sprit baptized. This caused controversy between the two leaders resulting in the right hand of fellowship being withdrawn from Mason and others of like belief. In 1907 Mason called for believers with like minds to meet him in Memphis, Tennessee where he reorganized the Church Of God In Christ as a Holiness-Pentecostal church. Mary Beth was now to be raised in Erie's Holy Trinity Church Of God In Christ under the leadership of Supt. J.D. Myers who was sent to the church by Bishop O.T. Jones, Sr. There her mother

[1] David E. Harrell Jr., *White Sects and Black Men in the Recent South* (Kingsport, TN: Vanderbilt UP, 1971) 95

became the Supervisor of Women, taught Adult Sunday School classes, and was a member of the Mother's Board.[2] Superintendent Willie Harris remembers Mother Lee as a no nonsense woman who as an usher "would walk around and make us spit our gum into her tissue."

Mother Lee was known for looking out for and responding to the needs of people. The 1920s seemingly would herald prosperity on a grand scale but by 1929 America would begin the longest economic downturn in its history starting with the stock market crash in October. It was called the Great Depression (1929-1939). Her mother was a woman who gave even out of her poverty and during the Depression their home was a haven for the homeless who rode the rails looking for work. The tramps, as they were called, repeatedly knocked on their door and the family shared whatever they had. It was a suffering time but also a happy time. Young people gathered in her kitchen where she shared milk, pie, love and advice. Her mother may have transferred her belief in the importance of civic involvement to Mary Beth as she observed her work with the *Erie Council of Churches* and *Church Women United*.

---

[2] Butler, Anthea *Women in the Church Of God In Christ Making a Sanctified World: University of North Carolina Press Chapel Hill, 2007, 2-3.* Butler defines church mothers as women who "set the cultural and behavioral patterns for the congregations...Whereas the tradition in many African American churches was for the church mother to be a mere figurehead...COGIC church mothers established their own organizational sphere within the confines of their denomination.

She grew up wanting to be a nurse and a missionary. After hearing a male missionary speak about Christ and how He suffered Mary Beth gave her life to the Lord at age 10. In the excitement of her pursuit in learning about the deeper things of her new life in Christ, as she matured she worked everywhere she could. A gifted speaker, older saints carried her to her speaking engagements. She also sang in the choir. The family followed the church going to district meetings and traveling to Philadelphia (where they met Bishop O.T Jones, Sr.) for the Church Of God In Christ Southeastern Jurisdiction Convocations.[3]   After the State was divided they went to Pittsburg for convocations.

Mary Beth was one of only two students of color in her class by the time she entered Strong Vincent High School. She was quick in her studies and determined to be at the top of her class in every subject. As a result she graduated at age 17 Valedictorian. Because of the systemic prejudice in Erie during that period, she was unaware that she was Valedictorian until thirty years after her graduation when she was featured as a speaker with five other students.

---

[3] The Church Of God In Christ hierarchy consists of local congregations. A District is made up of several churches and led by a District Superintendent. District Meetings are held bi-annually in the Spring and Fall. Districts make up Jurisdictions which are headed by a Jurisdictional Bishop. Jurisdictional meetings are held bi-annually in the Spring and Summer. At these gathering spirited services are held to refresh the souls of the saints, business reports are made regarding growth and other issues with financial reporting also being turned in. Bishop O.T. Jones, Sr., one of the first Jurisdictional Bishops appointed by Bishop C.H. Mason, was the founder of the Young People Willing Workers and Youth Congress.

Her father died before she graduated from Vincent and her mother didn't have funds to send her bright daughter to college. However, some of her teachers and assistant principal got together and raised the funds for a scholarship for the first semester and that was all she needed! In the early U.S. higher

Vincent Strong High School

education development, the College Board was formed to hold common college entrance tests. In 1901, the first examination included chemistry, and physics, and in 1902 botany was included. At the beginning of the 1944 school year this woman, who would transform lives and countries, boldly presented herself at Philadelphia's Temple University and was taken in though she never studied for or completed an entrance exam. She majored in Psychology. Although

Russell Conwell's founding vision was "to provide superior educational opportunities for academically talented and highly motivated students, regardless of their background or means," during the era Blacks were excluded from aspects of college life. For instance, Blacks could not live in the dormitory with White students, therefore she was taken in to live at one of the university's approved houses where women took in students. In addition to her core classes her natural ability to articulate was put to the test after she joined the Temple University's Debate Society.

While attending Temple, she joined the Holy Temple COGIC and served under the spiritual direction of Bishop and Mother O.T. Jones, Sr. O.T. Jr. had finished his undergraduate degree but was also at Temple studying for additional degrees. She was alone in a large city and the Jones family took her as one of their daughters. This relationship lasted a lifetime. (Each time Father and Mother Kennedy went back and forth around the world they stopped in Philadelphia to see them. Bishop Charles H. Mason was a frequent visitor to Philadelphia and at one of Bishop Jones Sr.'s services she asked Bishop Mason to bless her health and pray for her children. Bishop Mason prayed for the couple and then he prayed for all the children who were blessed by him.) The approved house she lived in was directly adjacent to the Jones' home and Mary Beth and

O.T Junior became close friends. In fact, the entire Holy Temple family embraced her. Sometimes she didn't have enough to eat and intuitively the saints invited her to one of three homes each Sunday where she enjoyed dinner. Bishop O.T. Jones Sr. was a champion of Youth and founded the Youth Department in 1912 in order for Church of God in Christ youth to be trained, to encourage one another and express themselves in positive ways. Mary Beth took part in all of the youth activities and enjoyed trips and church clubs.

She told no one at the church or school that attending Temple with very little funds was not easy. She discovered the tuition was only part of what she needed - there were books to buy, fees to pay, she had to have money to eat - and it was rough. Mary Elizabeth would not be deterred and threw herself into her studies, perhaps following the university's official motto — *Perseverantia Vincit*, or "Perseverance Conquers" she took every job she could to earn money. Summers she worked in Erie at odd jobs. On one winter job she sold coffee and was able to keep the money she made. Day after day she walked in the freezing streets of Philadelphia carrying the heavy bags of coffee. Never mind her cold fingers, with the money she made she could eat. Another job was to help someone clean. During this time of testing and preparation for greater work, she prayed a lot and became very consecrated. Toward the end of her university days she made minimum wages at Temple University Hospital where she worked in the supply room measuring medicine and distributing it by floors. The American Friends Society took them to Rockland State Hospital and she worked there for a while. Even more significantly, God gave her strength to finish college and she graduated in 1948 with a B.A. in Psychology.

K

Two

A Lifetime of Adventures

During World War II dive bombers like the *Dauntless* or *Apache* had a significant impact on the course of the war. Bombers were the ultimate long range heavy weapon. They provided the means to bypass the enemy's Army, Navy and natural barriers. They delivered massive firepower directly to the enemy's heart, striking its industry, vital resources, key military targets, and population centers, in order to significantly erode its strength in the battlefield and defeat it.

In addition to their main strategic role, the bombers also provided tactical air support and sometimes even close air support in the battlefield itself. On a national industrial scale, the provided a modern means to utilize technological advantage to balance the enemy's numerical advantage. Far more than tanks and warships, bombers provided the best means to concentrate great firepower in the hands of a small number of warriors, allowing the nation to rely more on its industry and less on millions of soldiers, and therefore pay the price of war with more money and less blood.

Because of these reasons, Great Britain and the United States produced the most advanced bombers and the largest bomber forces of World War II. The effectiveness of their bombers was very limited during the first years of the war by conservatism and technological difficulties, and by the fierce opposition of the enemy's air defense, but with gradual technological and tactical improvements, they eventually became a mighty and unstoppable force which crushed the enemy's war potential and contributed greatly to its defeat. [4]

With his degree and training in aeronautical engineering Chug worked on dive bombers trying to figure out a solution to why the aircraft's wings malfunctioned and fell off. At this point in his life, he was being drawn deeper into his personal

[4] http://www.2worldwar2.com/bombers.htm

relationship with Christ. As he studied spiritual things he felt it was wrong to design weapons to kill thousands of people. He made a decision to leave that lucrative career. As he searched for meaning, he began performing Peace work. The last group he worked with were the Quakers (Religious Society of Friends). As a Peace Church, the Society of Friends has always played a leading part in opposing preparations for war. The Peace Testimony, which is a very important Quaker principle, arose out of the belief in the in-dwelling Light or ``that of God'' in people. If that of God was a reality within oneself it would be denying the inner Spirit to take up arms against another.[5] It was while working for a Peace group in Philadelphia that the young White Quaker met the Black Temple University student, through her best friend Rose "Misa" Nakiyama a second generation Japanese American who was also a friend of Chug's. Chug and Mary Beth became fast friends during her senior year at Temple. She invited him to her church at Holy Temple. When

---

[5] http://quaker.org/friends.html

she found a job at the Rockland State Hospital through the American Friends Service Committee she and Chug became closer. It was at Rockland that Chug proposed to her. She was twenty two years old and had told everyone at Temple she would not marry until she was 30 because she wanted to see the world. She accepted his proposal reasoning that her mother had married at twenty-two. Little did she know that God would have the two of them see the world together while serving humanity.

Theirs was a genuine love match, though highly unusual for the time. (America's battle against interracial marriage had raged since the 17th century. In fact, prior to the California Supreme Court overturning what was called miscegenation laws in 1948, all southern states as well as Massachusetts and Pennsylvania made interracial laws illegal.) They married quietly in 1949 at a Quaker chapel in New York City, possibly due to the fact that all family members were not in favor of their marriage. Shortly thereafter they were led to relocate to Puerto Rico. The Commonwealth of Puerto Rico (Spanish for rich port) is a self-governing affiliate that shares all rights and obligations of U.S. citizenship. With its diverse cultural history (Puerto Ricans are descended from Spaniards, Africans and Native Americans) and Spanish and English the official languages, it was the right place for the young couple to begin their life together. "When Chug and I married it was very unusual for couples that weren't the same color to marry. We heard there wasn't prejudice in Puerto Rico and said we'd honeymoon there. While on the island we felt it was a good place to start our marriage and when we had children they would be better off there," Mother Kennedy remembered. She avoids the use of the word race because she feels that there is only one race, the *human race*. At their arrival, Charles found work in a government hospital and she taught at an elementary school until she was six months pregnant with their first child. (Two of their four children, Charles Jr. and Mary, would be born in Puerto Rico with Betsy and Grace being born in Africa.)

While her husband pursued his work, the youthful and always inquisitive Mary Beth set about learning medicine to prepare her for midwifery on the mission field. The Lord continued to prepare the couple for missions by allowing them to live with people where they learned to speak Spanish fluently. The Lord would further prepare them while in Puerto Rico by directing them to join a multicultural interdenominational church. There they met a group of missionaries who invited them to live with them. The year they were there they worshipped God, joined a special prayer group with one of the couples, brought others into the Kingdom through teaching the Word, served the people and learned missions work with Mary Beth being trained by a doctor in taking blood pressure, midwifery and dispensing medicine. They served as missionaries in Puerto Rico for five years.

God had plans to bring them back home and, through her Church Of God In Christ roots, move them further into missions work. Although she initially had doubts, it was in Puerto Rico that the Lord called them into international missions.

One Sunday my daughter was sick and she and I stayed home from church. I was having my own private devotion and as I prayed [I saw] the shape of Africa. A man standing on the continent of Africa said "come over and help us."

I said that can't be real but yet I knew that God had spoken. And we were in such a nice place; the place was perfect to bring up children. It had a great big enclosed place where our children and the other missionary's children could play and it was just perfect from a human point of view. But I just knew the Lord had called and I didn't want to change, I didn't want to move, I didn't want to go somewhere else. I didn't know what Africa would be like. I told Chug and he counseled me to pray. He would pray with me. Every

time I'd open my Bible or hymn book [I'd read] about missions.
Chug said if that what the Lord is saying we'll go.

The couple made plans to save money to go to Africa. They packed up everything they could bring back to the mainland and gave everything else away. She wrote to her friend O.T. Jones, Jr. and told him that God had called them to Africa. "He was very happy about it." After moving in with her mother, Elder Kennedy returned to work as an engineer at Electroweld and American Sterilizer Company, specializing in stress analysis and earning several patents and professional awards. The couple received further missionary training in 1955, the year before they left for Africa. Charles also served as a minister to the Hispanic migrant farm workers for the Council of Churches.

Answering The Call to Africa and The World

In the 21st century global communication is taken for granted. Powerful technology flashes news of tsunamis across television and iPad screens within hours of occurrence and for science aficionados high powered cameras such as Hubble's send detailed and graceful images of distant galaxies billions of light years away from the Earth. Discovery of isolated people groups are documented through the History Channel within months of contact.

Of course it has not always been so. Pioneer Church Of God In Christ International Missionaries, intentional in their desire to communicate events taking place on foreign fields sent letters to *The Whole Truth* of their successes.[6] Names of Church Of God In Christ international missionaries were listed in the back pages of Sunday School books along with their locations of service. Once they made up their mind to follow God's leading, Chug and Mary Beth retrieved an old Sunday School book and saw Mother Martha Barber's name and wrote to her. Although the only Church Of God In Christ foreign missionary she had seen was Mother Dorothy Webster Exume, foreign missionary to Haiti, they contacted Mother Barber who responded that she'd like them to come to the fertile country of Liberia, West Africa. It was located in a dense tropical rain forest, full of trees yielding valuable lumber or dyestuffs, and home to all kinds of dangerous animals.[7] The contact set in motion a lifetime of helping to redeem individuals from natural poverty and spiritual lack.

Liberia has a long history of Christian activity. It was fertile ground for the Gospel and Methodist, Baptist and Catholic Churches served there for many years prior to the Church Of God In Christ's entrance. Bishop Richard Allen, founder of the African Methodist Episcopal Church, had established the Haytian Emigration Society of Coloured People formed as a

---

[6]The Whole Truth Newspaper was used to inform congregations of healings, testimonies and organizational development. Formerly called "Truth "in the 1890s, the name changed after the 1907 reorganization.

[7] Williams Goodson, Glenda, *Royalty Unveiled* , 2011 Lancaster: HCM Publishing, 112

protest against segregation in 1787[8] and sent missionaries. And two Assemblies of God "colored" ministers Alexander and Margret Howard, set sail for Liberia in 1920.[9]

Martha Barber journeyed to Africa from Chicago. She arrived at Cape Palmas, West Africa on March 28, 1946. Barber was sent by International Supervisor Mother Lizzie Robinson to Church Of God In Christ's Liberian Tugbaken Mission to assist the first Church Of God In Christ missionary to Africa, Mother Elizabeth White. Elizabeth White, the first official COGIC missionary to Africa, male or female, began her work under the banner of the Assemblies of God in the 1920s. The core of her responsibility was ensuring that the Liberian was uplifted through education, sharing knowledge of medical advancements and building churches and orphanages. Even more important, entire villages were introduced to the saving grace of Jesus Christ. The early missionaries performed marriage ceremonies, presided over funerals and baptized new converts.

Mother Kennedy was ready to go to Africa to resume the mission work she and her husband had started in Puerto Rico.

---

[8] ibid, 35

[9] http://www.pe.ag.org/articles/index_2011.cfm?targetBay=ff479279-680e-4b02-ba0b-8f9ff830e632&Process=DisplayArticle&RSS_RSSContentID=18212&RSS_OriginatingRSSFeedID=4677&RSS_Source=

But first they were required to obtain permission from the national church. She traveled by bus and arrived in Memphis to attend the 1956 Holy Convocation. (The annual convocation began in 1907 when Church Of God In Christ founder Bishop Charles Harrison Mason called for all like believers to meet him in Memphis for 20 days from November 25 to December 14. This time was chosen because the majority of the church's adherents lived in the farming districts of Tennessee, Arkansas and Mississippi and after harvesting their crops they could support a national meeting.)

In Memphis she was vetted by the Missions Board and International Supervisor of Women, Mother Lillian Brooks Coffey, who succeeded Mother Robinson at her death in 1945. The Kennedy's were approved although, she recalled, "I didn't understand why we had to meet with them and I guess I had an attitude. The Missions Board was under the Department of Women and Mother Coffey didn't necessarily like my attitude which was *I'm* the one going to Africa and *you're* not, but when you're in your twenties...." The energetic and competent couple were the first missions' couple the Church Of God In Christ sent out. Mother Kennedy was naïve, not knowing there was no coordinated financial policy for sustaining missionaries. For years, the Church Of God In Christ has had an interesting custom that some feel needs to

be discontinued: They require those going out on the foreign field to raise their own fare to serve God and serve the church. (Though initially they didn't know about fundraising and partnering during furloughs, as they ventured deeper into the work of missions, they would find that there were those willing to partner with them both in prayer and in finances.) The Kennedy's put aside money each week for the steamship and were scheduled to leave in January 1957. They had one problem— they had only saved enough for one ticket. Mother Kennedy has been described as a strong willed, dynamic, charismatic, and beautiful person who can charm the socks off of anyone. Sometimes prone to impatience, her dogged determination was to get to West Africa with her entire family. What could be done? Never one to be defeated when she set her mind to something, the emboldened Mary Beth took a shortcut straight to power by contacting the steamship's CEO and convincing him to help them.

I checked and we had enough money for one person to go. That was all. I said if we skimp here and skimp there we might finally get enough for two people. But that was still Elder Kennedy's and my fare and we had two children and what was supposed to happen about that? So the Lord just gave me and I wrote to the owner, the

CEO of the Farrell Steamship Line.[10] I said the Lord has called us to go to Africa and that we both were highly qualified and that we could get good jobs here in the States. But we felt that there was a tremendous need over in Africa and we were willing to sacrifice that and go to Africa. But we did not have the money for four people. If they would let us just be in the same stateroom, the children could sleep in there with us. And we would give them food from our plate. And just let them go free.[11]

Her argument prevailed and as a result of her faith all tickets were delivered. They packed the few things they had left included Father Kennedy's precious bike. All four Kennedys arrived at the New York Harbor with four full fare tickets for the entire family provided by the owner with the children having their own stateroom. Someone pointed out the owner of the line, who sat in a boat watching them board possibly to get a glimpse of the woman who had the chutzpah to ask for free tickets. In her book, *A Visit to Wissikeh* Mary Kennedy describes that on the 19 to 20 day voyage none of them became seasick.

---

[10] God's favor was with the Kennedy's. James Farrell, Sr., owned one of the best known of the large U.S.-flagged shipping companies back in the post-Second World War era. In the late 1940s, Farrell not only had a good-sized fleet of freighters, but two rather luxurious passenger-cargo liners, as well. James A. Farrell Sr. had two sons to whom he imparted his shipping knowledge and business savvy. Both sons, John and James Jr., went on to operate two of the three major shipping investments. The two were able to create a powerful management team and operated the main U.S. flag and passenger service between Africa and the United States. http://www.farrelllines.com/history.php , http://www.sshsa.org/publications/powerships.html

[11] Williams Goodson, Glenda, *Royalty Unveiled Lancaster:* HCM Publishing, 136

The Church Of God In Christ owned three missions stations in Liberia: Tugbakeh, Monolu and Wissekeh. Ships did not go to Cape Palmas so they safely completed the first leg of their journey when they stepped off the boat in Monrovia. Next they flew four hours from Monrovia to Harper, the capital of Maryland County and its largest city. They did not know what to expect culturally. Elder Kennedy—compassionate, self-assured, erudite, with a great ability of transcendence—with limited exposure to the continent (only from old Tarzan movies) had particular concern because of his color.

They moved further into the interior on hardwood seats placed in the back of trucks that served as transportation over muddy paths to Cape Palmas. Mother Kennedy explained that when water rolled over the swollen river, it was almost impossible to navigate.

If the river's up you don't cross and things like that. It's very, very underdeveloped. See, Liberians proudly say, and it's something to be proud of, that they were never subject to anybody. That they were never a colony, that they've always been free. But the fact that they've always been free they didn't have that money coming in to fix the place. And so Congo where I am Supervisor is far, far more advanced than Liberia because the Belgiums were there. They were very cruel and they slaughtered people, they killed people, they cut off people's hands but they built roads. You can get from one place to another in Congo. Not with the greatest of ease. It's not like the U.S. but they have good roads and a lot of traffic and that sort of thing. Whereas in Liberia, you get on the back of a truck, you have to ride on back of the trucks on hardwood seats, not in the cab. That's their bus. That's their way of transporting people.

As they approached the Tugbaken Mission the weight of their belongings caused the bridge to collapse and the front of the truck crashed through and fell over the bridge. At the sound of the crash the children from the mission campus were first to arrive at the accident scene. Mother Kennedy noted, "They came pouring out of the houses and down the hill to meet us...so happy to see us. And Elder Kennedy said that his fears of Africa evaporated at that point. He wasn't afraid anymore, ever."[12]

They finally arrived at Tugbaken in January. The Mission children unloaded the trucks and Mother Barber gave the family rooms to sleep in. Now Mother Kennedy wondered if Church Of God In Christ officials were right in asking them to leave their children. When they arrived in Liberia Charles Jr. was six years old and Mary was four. She prayed and asked

---

[12]Ibid. 139

God to help them in their ability to experience a smooth adjustment period.[13]

They served at the Tugbaken Mission with Mother Barber one year. Mother Kennedy taught in the school and provided medical services. Elder Kennedy worked with the four ordained elders affiliated with the missions, each of which exhibited a high level of intelligence. He provided them with further religious instruction in areas such as the ordinances of the church after which they began serving Holy Communion.

During that year they became acquainted with the work of foreign missions, gained knowledge of local customs, and made adjustments to the African culture. Mother Barber was very strict, reserved, and dedicated. She had a saying, *Duty Bound*. As a young woman Mother Kennedy thought the motive of one's service should be love, however, as she grew older she realized that whatever God has given a person to do it was their duty to perform it. Though it's always better to do things from love at least if doing them through duty the work

---

[13] Most of the early missionaries sent out by the Church Of God In Christ were single females. Charles and Mary Beth Kennedy presented a novelty in that they were the first couple COGIC sent out and officials were reluctant for them to take the children. The decision for children going on the foreign field was uncommon for the period among COGIC adherents and an alternative offer was to send the Kennedy children to Saints in Lexington with Dr. Arenia Mallory. They responded that when God called them to Africa He knew we had children and refused to leave their children in the States.

is being done. The Kennedy's taught in the school and worked in the church at Tugbaken.

After that first eventful year, a group of African nationals walked fifteen miles to Tugbakeh and asked them to come and examine the abandoned Wissikeh Mission Station, founded by the first Church Of God In Christ missionary to Africa, Mother Elizabeth White. Elizabeth White, the first official COGIC missionary to Africa, male or female, began her work under the banner of the Assemblies of God in the 1920s. After returning to the United States, she joined the Church Of God In Christ and was sent back to Liberia 1929-1930 under the COGIC banner.[14] The men, Jeremiah and Daniel Tobe, said it was far in the interior and they had missionaries before and they wanted missionaries to return. Although there was nothing there at that time, not even a residence for a missionary, upon his return Father Kennedy stated he saw the possibilities.

Though it would be a difficult task, they decided to go and

---

[14] [14]Williams Goodson, Glenda, *Royalty Unveiled* , 2011 Lancaster: HCM Publishing, 110

Father Kennedy watches as his children pose with Wissikeh friends

prepared to leave Tugbaken. On December 4, 1957 the family moved deep into the interior to the old Wissikeh Mission Station. It was very, very rugged and inaccessible by motor vehicle. With Wissikeh far away from civilization, a person walked or was carried in a hammock the fifteen miles into the high bush. Mother Kennedy, then in her twenties and in fairly good health, felt no one should have to carry her and began to walk. She found that although being carried in a hammock was rough it was better than walking. Upon their arrival at the abandoned site they discovered that the former missionary home was uninhabitable. A building erected by Mother White was almost totally destroyed. There were four walls that were standing but not a roof and no windows or doors or steps. Trees were growing up inside the building that was high as the building itself and so was totally unlivable for a missionary residence or anyone else. The roof was gone, the floor, doors and windows were rotted. Trees grew thirty feet high within the moss-covered block walls. They had no home. However, knowing that God had sent them, they took six or seven students with them and served in the jungle. They lived with Pastor Jika White and his wife in their mud hut until their mud house could be built.

Around the time the family were in the third year of progress rebuilding the Wissikeh station, U.S. President John F. Kennedy called the nation and its youth to serve the world by offering technological, educational and humanitarian assistance to poorer countries. He chose Sergeant Shriver to head one of these, the U.S. Peace Corps, and agency workers fanned out across the globe in places like Liberia. However, Wissekeh was so remote that even the Peace Corps thought it was too dangerous to put their people.[15] When the season for annual rains arrived, the waters rose and no one could get from Wissekeh unless they swam. They were cut off from the rest of the world, but Mother Kennedy explained they were "never cut off from God."

---

[15]Williams Goodson, Glenda, *Royalty Unveiled* , 2011 Lancaster: HCM Publishing, 143

During their tenure in Liberia the Kennedys founded the only Church Of God In Christ high school in Liberia as well as an elementary school and a Bible School. They even built a clinic which furnished the only medical care in a nine hundred square mile radius.

The work at Wissikeh was filled with challenges. There were real dangers living in the jungles of West Africa. Wissikeh means nest of witches and the couple fought spiritual battles against very strong superstition and witchcraft. God was with the missionaries when the witches utilized various strategies in attempts to frighten the couple away. "Elder Kennedy, would not jump into any situation without thinking things out," Mother Kennedy recalled. Once the witches harassed them by blowing on human skulls to make loud noises. In the wake of the provocation, the issue became one of faith to stand down the enemy. Pa Kennedy told his wife that the next time she heard them to wake him up. "Chug, who was of small stature, got three big strong men to accompany him to demand that they cease. Our son was about 7 or 8 and accompanied his dad down the path following the sound of the skull horns. They carried a brand new flashlight that shone about three city blocks. Nothing is dark like an African night. And all of a sudden the flashlight went out and all they had were their machetes. They didn't know if those who were

34

blowing the skull horns had machetes. Looking from the window I grabbed a lantern and went out where they were. Their next step would have been on a deadly scorpion.

The couple had the loyalty, compassion and goodwill of many Liberian nationals who they trained in news ways to care for their own. One of the young men who was a Sunday School student was especially adept at nursing. He built his own clinic made of mud, built shelves and served the people. With the entrance of Christian missionaries cannibalism, with people eating people, attempts were made to eradicate the ancient tradition yet the practice was an actual occurrence. Years after their return to the United States, they were informed that this young man had been killed and sacrificed. During the period when Charles Jr., was just beginning puberty with its rush of hormones accompanied by confusing emotions. Yet, his sense of responsibility to the cause of Christ caused him to go out into the jungle with his friend where he could have been snatched and eaten. Indeed Charles Jr. displayed a deep spiritually, and was particularly drawn to venture deeper into the jungle to tell the nationals about the love and power of Jesus Christ.

Alfred, John and I would go on a Sunday to carry the gospel to a little bit more remote part of Liberia. As a result the father or uncle of two of the boys, who was an accomplished witch man, ended up accepting Christ and he became the pastor of the church several years later after Paul White had passed.

The practitioner had killed numerous people and he would predict to them what was going to happen. The witch man was well respected and feared, he had three wives, was very accomplished and very proficient in what he did. The man also knew country medicine. When a snake bit someone he knew how to get the poison out. But Charles made an impact in that village. After he got saved, by his own admission he testified that when Charles and the others came and preached to him, he thought to himself that he should have been preaching to them. He became a very, very powerful force for God in that community.

Confronting spiritual darkness was tantamount to inviting trouble in spiritual realms. Yet Elder Kennedy went throughout nearby villages freeing people from the bondage of Satan and witchcraft, boldly confronting witch doctors, baptizing some three hundred persons and ordaining elders as he had been given authority to do. A pressing problem was the lack of formal education in the villages needed to equip nationals for the world outside the villages. They heeded the call and established several additional elementary schools and clinics in surrounding villages and trained many local mission people as ministers, teachers and medical workers. The Liberian experience would serve him well as they journeyed throughout the world in ministry.

Bishop Vincent Matthews provides an accurate assessment of the inspiration the Kennedy's invoke. By his account, as he observed the behavior of Father Kennedy and assessed his ability to transcend cultural and spiritual obstacles to get the job done he was motivated to do more. "I NEVER saw him as a White man. In fact I never even recognized race with him. He was able to transcend triviality and go straight to the core of matters and issues. Going on a trip later with them deep into the DRC jungle where there are only paths made me determined to do more. They squeezed more out of a week in their life in their 70's than most people get from an entire life. This is not a hyperbolic statement, it is fact!!!! I witnessed it!!!!!"

Their initial foray into the world outside the United States was no coincidence. After leaving Puerto Rico, they served seven years at Wissekeh and God was faithful. Mother Kennedy: The most important thing to remember is God's faithfulness. He has never failed us for all these years. The blessings of our convictions has allowed us with the testimony to tell our children and many others of His faithfulness. It is only when we trust God and we put our full confidence in Him, that He will not fail us.

The church, whether in developing countries or First World countries, must always upgrade the life of the community. Mother Kennedy immediately established a school, *Lee Elementary* named for her mother, by using the shade of a large tree as her classroom. Later the school was expanded and students were taught in grades 1-12. Despite sometimes finding themselves in the midst of grave danger they rebuilt the mission, many were saved and the Kennedys also built a church. Their daily routine consisted of Morning Prayer at 6:00 a.m. Father Kennedy's engineering background came in handy as he designed the buildings.

Some Liberian national's admiration for the Kennedy's approached the reverential. Jessie Brown is the wife of the late Bishop Abraham Brown, Prelate of the West Africa Ivory Coast Ecclesiastical Jurisdiction. She grew up at the Wissikeh Mission Station and says she will be forever thankful for the entrance of the couple into the Wissikeh community. "Pa Chug was so humble. He would make a bed out of anything and sleep on the floor. Whatever we cooked they ate anything we had. They left their good home and flushed toilets to go and build toilets outside. Some of us didn't know about God.

When I say dark country I mean no God. Missionaries came there, suffered there, and spent their money. That's how some of us got saved. Not only teaching us about God but they brought us here in the great country of America. Thank God for the Church Of God In Christ. I will forever be Church Of God In Christ because of the missionaries. Thank God for the missionaries. They have a big star up there." Many former students relocated to the United States while others returned to help rebuild their country.

Significantly, their holistic approach to serving included providing quality health care. The medical training Mother Kennedy received in Puerto Rico along with courses taken in the United States as a Licensed Practical Nurse came in handy as she used her skills to heal those having tropical diseases such as malaria, tuberculosis, snakebites or hookworms. Mentoring comes in many forms and the couple, ever believing that knowledge must be passed on, trained mission students' basic nursing such as how to take temperatures and how to take blood pressure.

Daughter Betsy was born in Liberia and the family lived there until she was six. She remembers a time when her mother's medical training came in handy,

In Liberia, I remember having a huge sore on my big toe that

wouldn't heal - for months on end. It was getting infected, and the sore was all the way to the bone. (I still have a large scar.) I remember Mom putting some sulfa power on it that finally did the trick in healing it. The point being that in so many situations they faced, they had to be creative and use the limited resources that were available to fix the problems.

Elder Kennedy, being very good at whatever he attempted, planted a beautiful farm with a wide variety of vegetables. The missions students helped, had their own part and the garden flourished. There was one hitch: Wissikeh had more cows than anywhere around because cows were a measure of wealth. The people from the town of Harper or other areas of the town were quick to capitalize on the fact that they could drive their cows back into the jungle to graze and they would not have to take care of them. The cows broke down the fences and ate Father Kennedy's entire crop. Father Kennedy was an extremely self-possessed man who didn't believe in war or fighting but was not afraid to stand up for what he believed was right. He was very annoyed but rebuilt the fence telling the townspeople to keep the cows out of the garden because they were responsible for taking care of them.

The third time the farm was destroyed they went on a fast. In a show of strength, Father Kennedy, Mother Kennedy and their children, accompanied by all the mission children and young people, went into Wissikeh and stopped in the middle of the town and stayed there. The townspeople were afraid of evil spirits they thought would come in the dark and begged the group to leave. They refused and stayed there all night fasting. The next day came and the townspeople came to see what could be done to redeem the situation. Since they didn't confirm the cows would be constrained, the group stayed and kept fasting.

Mother Kennedy had a heart condition and grew weak. The townspeople was afraid she would die and, detailing their side of the issue, sent for Mother Barber who walked the fifteen miles from Tugbaken. Father Kennedy was stubborn and could not be persuaded to leave until he had an agreement that they would rebuild the fence. Mother Barber parlayed with them and the fence was subsequently repaired.

After leaving Africa, they returned to the United States but their ministry—both home and abroad— did not end. They made many short term trips to Liberia where the children would become reacquainted with their Liberian brothers and sisters. Betsey was old enough to recall readjusting to Third World conditions.

Lori and I, as teenagers, were in Liberia with Mom and Dad on a missions trip. We shared a bed, safely tucked in under the mosquito net, but Lori kept feeling something move in the mattress! We were afraid that it was a snake, but we had been taught to not get out of the bed without light be able to see around us. Needless to mention, we were quite loud in our calls for help. But no sense in calling Mom, it was Dad we yelled for! (It turned out to be a mouse.)

The couple along with family and team members, whether sending funds through their network to persecuted Christians in unnamed countries, working in Ghanaian refugee camps, or providing needed funds for medical supplies in Communist countries, have ministered in over twenty-seven countries some of which are shown below.

Some Countries the Kennedy's Have Ministered in

Liberia
Haiti
Cuba
Democratic Republic of Congo
South Africa
Ivory Coast
Tanzania
Sierra Leone
Ghana
Zambia
Dominican Republic
South America

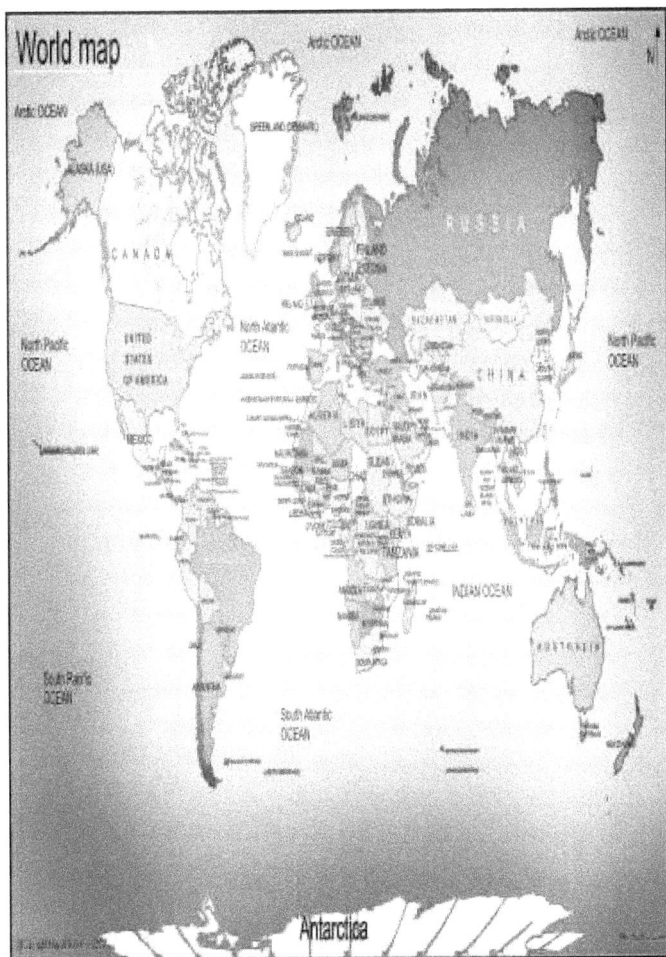

World map

K

Four

He Who Stands Alone -- She Who Conquers

Whether we believe it or not, purpose is connected to naming. Beginning with biblical texts, a custom of many people groups is to prophetically pronounce names on individuals as a guiding principle of who they are and who they would become: Years after Jacob used deceit against his brother for the birthright and blessing, as a mature man ready to confront Esau his name was changed to Israel.

By the time they celebrated their 50th wedding anniversary the Kennedy's had lived out the names given them years before by the Liberians. He was called Dote, which means *"He stands alone"* and she was named Kworo, *"she who conquers."* When one is inspired by a great purpose thoughts of failure may enter consciousness but the individual does not allow negativity to linger. The couple, as most Christians who would have greatness ascribed to them, lived out the text that says with God all things are possible. As a result of reaching out to countless numbers with the Gospel of the Lord Jesus Christ and providing training, education, health care, agriculture, carpentry, and much more they found themselves to be greater persons that they ever dreamed.

Veni Vidi Vici. Yet as they aged and reflected upon their truly exceptional life, the pair saw the need for legacy. Having formed alliances over the years, their legacy of love would continue to make a positive impact upon the world. They ramped up efforts to pour into others with the missionary impulse to continue the work of The Great Commission. Current International Prayer and Bible Band Topic Writer (and former Supervisor of Brazil) Supervisor Lee Van Zandt has worked as an international missionary since she was saved under the late Haitian pioneer missionary Dr. Dorothy Webster Exume. She met the Kennedy's in the 1960s. Later, she traveled with them on a Youth on a Mission trip to Mexico. The wisdom of the couple proved evident as valuable lessons such as inter-cultural sensitivity and others that could only be learned on location, were shared.

To know Mother Kennedy is to love her. She shared so many things with me during that trip. I will never forget her advice to "always find out as much as you can about the country you are serving – the water situation, the monetary system, the country's religions, the culture – because the people will know...if you are real or not."

While it is a given for individuals serving internationally to be prepared for emergencies, Supervisor Van Zandt explained Mother Kennedy's novel suggestions such as the fact that *bobbie pins come in handy, needles and thread, safety pins [come in handy [but] one of the most profound things she shared on that trip was to love the people, the children and the seniors. When we are serving we must remember that everything we do is to be about missions. Their lives reflected that. She could go into warring countries and be effective in her assignment because she would listen for God to tell her what to do, what to wear, who to contact. She never let anything stop her from completing her assignment."*

One of the couple's long desires was for other couples to think differently about their lives and embrace the call to the mission field. Since their return from Liberia, there had not been a Church Of God In Christ family serving full time in that area and they longed to see God bring that prayer to pass. In His own time and infinite wisdom, God was preparing someone in the persons of Vincent and Sharon Matthews.

Currently, the newly appointed President of Church Of God In Christ Global Missions, Bishop Vincent Matthews, travels the globe as he builds on the foundation of the pioneers and brings innovative ideas to further organize this vital part of Church Of God In Christ ministry. He recalls the lessons shared from those he refers to as "heroes of the faith" and the powerful impact they had on his ministry and family.

I set up a meeting at the convocation in 2002 after service in the Cook Convention Center. We were in awe of their experience and reputation. Elder Kennedy profoundly warned us to count the costs and be certain to have support because things could be difficult. They told us how they miraculously received money to board a voyage to Liberia. They also told us to be careful with our children and a lot of other specific things that no one had ever considered.

Working on the foreign field is not for the fainthearted, especially in war torn countries. The legacy of trailblazers includes passing on the idea that courage plays a major part of the international missionary's life. Though external occurrences outside their sphere of influence occurred, they never forgot their African family of students and friends. From 1989 through 2003, Liberia was held in the grip of two terrible civil wars which raged throughout the entire country. They visited the nation annually, even during the war years.

"Mom and dad had a special kind of relationship that very few people have," says their oldest daughter Mary. Their relationship with God and close relationship with one another would sustain them during all the war years as the pair worked together to forward the work through Missions of mercy and short-term mission trips, jointly sponsored by the Community of Caring and the Church Of God In Christ.

In the Southwest, the town of Blonikeh where Mother Elizabeth White began the work of Church Of God In Christ Church in Africa, was burned to the ground. Nothing remained of the former missions. Both UPC and Church Of God In Christ Tugbakeh Mission and Monalu Mission sustained substantial damage but the mission stations can be, and are in the process of being, rebuilt. Holy Temple Church Of God In Christ was bombed and completely ruined but was the only Church Of God In Christ Church in the Northwest to suffer severe damage. Bishop Nyema and the Church Of God In Christ Youth On A Mission directed by Dr. June Rivers rebuilt the mother church, Holy Temple, in Monrovia. Wissikeh Mission, because of its remote location, sustained no real damage to the buildings although the people suffered terribly from marauding soldiers, hunger and illness.

For Father Kennedy it sometimes seemed that he stood alone

in his and his wife's desire to pave the way for future generations to experience a brighter future in America and abroad. God kept them safe although they risked their lives numerous times, going behind rebel lines when necessary, in order to reach the Church Of God In Christ mission stations with food and medicines. These activities were designed to bring humanitarian (as well as spiritual) aid to the suffering thousands. Usually five to eight highly skilled persons made these Missions of Mercy trips, taking in badly needed medical supplies, food and money and preaching the Gospel. Approximately $250,000 worth of supplies was taken into the country during those terrible years. At the height of the war, 1,100 starving persons were fed daily under the auspices of the Community of Caring and the Bethel Temple Church Of God In Christ (Elder S. Tosha Browne, pastor). Recognizing their purpose and foresight, the United Nations helped in this program.

In choosing to live a life in missions activities, sometimes unleashing a positive mental attitude into the world was challenging in light of the real danger to be reckoned with in much of the areas they served in. Despite the difficulty, they yet kept moving forward in their assignment. In Haiti, God's hand of protection was upon them once again. Recalls Betsy, "On one trip, my husband went by himself to Haiti with my parents. I was to join them later in the Dominican Republic. They were conducting a clinic at one of the local churches, and rioting broke out and moved into the area where they were. My husband, who is a retired army officer, looked up and saw that the rioters were carrying guns! He rushed and told my parents to get out of the line of sight, and right at that time, the rioters started shooting!! Bullets flew by, but thankfully, no one was hurt."

Continuing to advance in years, they began opening the trips to others who wanted the experience of working on the mission field. Marva Cromartie Nyema recalled that on her first mission trip to Haiti, like John Mark, she left the trip early. After her call to international missions work, at the urging of International Missions President Bishop Carlos Moody, she returned to Haiti with the couple in 1986. Later, Nyema accompanied the Kennedys on other mission trips where they guided, trained and mentored her through the customs, relationships and power structures that constituted success in international missions work on the field and, ironically, the labyrinth of church politics at home.

Missions workers can expect to risk their lives and health in areas besides war. Not only do those on the field brave horrific external threats but they know that current emergencies are not the last emergency. The late Elder Havious Green of Detroit, a longtime supporter of missions, traveled with the couple on several occasions to DRC and Zambia. His daughter, Dr. June Rivers (who has served as the COGIC Youth on a Mission leader for almost twenty-five years)[16] chronicles that once in the DRC her father almost died. "On one such visit, the temperature was very hot so Mother Kennedy and her husband, Elder Charles Kennedy travelled from one village to the next village in hammocks carried by nationals. Elder Green, an athletic and independent person, decided to run the distance to the next village. A successful athlete in college, he had remained physically fit most of his life. However, when he arrived at the next village, he exhibited symptoms of dehydration due to the physical exertion and the diuretic which he took as a part of his medications for high blood pressure. Consequently, Mother Kennedy sprang into action by mixing the appropriate amounts of sugar and salt in water and then had Elder Green to drink the mixture which revived him and surely saved his life." After much prayer, he recovered. He would later build a house for Bishop Mayuke with a flushable toilet!

---

[16] Youth on a Mission is an integral asset to the COGIC mission. It was established by Bishop Carlis L. Moody, (Department of Missions President 1973-2015) as a ministry of young people visiting the mission field to serve each summer.

Fatigue and disillusionment could further cause the fight against adversity in order to serve humanity to wane. Still, the Kennedy's seemed tireless and served individuals in need of their help well in the evenings many times under extreme circumstances. As missions workers they wished a smooth transition in transferring the work to those under their tutelage and challenged neophyte workers in strategic areas.

Worldwide, millions of individuals are disabled by Hansen's disease (leprosy) each year. During the early days of their Liberian ministry the requests for food, medical aid, education and knowledge of the big God was tremendous. They were concerned that they would not physically be able to keep up with the demands. Even more worrying, a request was made for the mother of small children to minister at a leper colony. Mother Kennedy struggled within herself to overcome fear and misgivings about the disease being transmitted to her. Later, armed with knowledge that the disease is not highly infectious and curable, she insisted that mentees move beyond fear. According to Nyema, "When she shared with me that we were going to a leprosy camp, I was scared and volunteered to stay at a village until they returned but she told me no. Therefore, I mustered strength with the help of the Lord, to go with them." As the newly appointed missionary to the COGIC Tugbakah Mission Station, the pair provided valuable information as Nyema prepared for the trip.

When it was time for me to go as a full time missionary to Liberia, the Kennedy's suggested that I purchase a filter cup to filter water. Even though the water did not taste good to me once it was filtered, I would filter the water and also boil the water. Since I was not in the medical field, they also suggested I purchase a book to help when there is no doctor in the village. This book taught me how to recognize various diseases and how to treat people.

The mission assignment in the 1950s has caused the Kennedy's minister in over 27 countries. Throughout the years, they have found that making a conscious decision to focus on solutions brought more results than bewailing the challenge. Because of this focus they were enabled to courageously carry the Good News of Jesus Christ to places where it was dangerous to go but God granted them favor.

After World War II, former allies, mainly the United States and the USSR, entered what has been termed the Cold War (1945-1980). During the Cold War the mutual distrust between the two superpowers resulted in an international power struggle over beliefs and ideology. Relations between the two were tense and ordeals such as the Bay of Pigs Cuban Missile Crisis only caused further estrangement. The Iron

Russian folklore character presented to Mother Kennedy made by inmates when Kennedy's visited Russian prison during Cold War circa 1960

Curtain seemed to be impenetrable and the society was closely controlled. There were restrictions on American travel to the USSR and USSR citizen travel to the United States. Those traveling to the Soviet Union could only travel to cities with populations more than 100,000. Yet, there was those behind the Iron Curtain in need of natural and spiritual assistance. During the mid-1950s, after Stalin's death, travel between the two countries became less restricted. They Kennedy's entered Russia during the 1960s to provide aid. While there, they lived with a Russian Christian who did not speak English and they did not speak her language. Somehow they communicated and while there the couple ministered in a hospital and a Russian prison.

Their mission trips declined but their legacy continues through their children and others they have trained and nurtured. Bishop Matthews remembers several trips the power couple made to South Africa, however, it was their eventful first trip the neophyte international missionaries would observe the experienced couple's resiliency in the face of adverse circumstances, Father Kennedy's profundity in sharing the gospel and Mother Kennedy's giftings particularly in the linguistics' area.

Sharon cooked more food that we'd had since leaving America. I wondered aloud where she got all the money. During dinner Elder Kennedy began to cry saying it was just at 50 years later after they had gone on the field that the next missions family was now on the field. I felt this awesome sense of historical responsibility...a passing of the baton. We talked until about 1am about the call to serve God. This is when Eld Kennedy was in his element with his profundity and prophetic advice. I soaked it all up while noting the irony that it took so long for another family to move and serve God cross culturally through COGIC Missions.

Spurred on by the visit, after bidding the team farewell Bishop Matthews preached impacting the world with the Great Commission to his congregation that had grown from six to 65 in one year. His church was about to learn that the Sovereign God would use the Kennedy's to usher in a dynamic explosion and push them toward greater outreach ministry.

I was at the Altar call about to sign up soldiers to GO and evangelize with me on the upcoming week when all of a sudden in walks Bishop Girardeau Nesbitt, the Kennedy's and those traveling with them 5 hours after they left. It seems the driver I hired only knew his circular route and had no idea where the airport was located and was lost for that entire time!!!!! They walked in with suitcases filling the back of our small church. I cancelled the altar call and called a revival to begin that very night. I said this was a sign from that Lord that the "keepers of the Great Commission" walked in at that very moment!!! We would have revival services until they left on the next plane going to DRC. I was not going to squander that opportunity. I then mobilized our baby saints to go out and get people to come to church at this short notice. Some said people would not come, but I said God sent us a sign...the Kennedys!!!! We had 2 services a day AND health clinic and many were saved.

This is when I first learned that Mother Kennedy is a true linguist! She began to pick up the languages being spoken and sang and use the words effortlessly. She has a gift for language. She even sang songs in Sotho and Zulu even though she had never heard them before....she just caught on in microseconds!

Indeed, the Kennedy's represent stability in an increasingly chaotic world. As late as 2010 Mother Kennedy yet traveled globally to serve humanity.

On January 12, 2010 a large scale 7.0 magnitude earthquake struck in Haiti. Deaths were estimated from 230,000 to 310,000 and 300,000 were injured. As estimated 1.5 million were displaced and aid came from around the world. The ever present missionary impulse within Mother Kennedy caused her to join others on their way to Haiti by way of the Dominican Republic. As they waited for the arrival of the rest of their team, one of the volunteers talked with a young American (whose parents were missionaries) who told them about a nearby Haitian settlement. With the assistance of a local artist as guide, Mother Kennedy led the group to the displaced community. After a brief religious service she encouraged the refugees that the group would return the next day along with their medical team

Because of the danger in the Haitian infrastructure, it was decided that the wheelchair bound Mother Kennedy could not go into Haiti and she had to remain in the Dominican Republic. What did she do because of this challenge to her mission that she could not control? She chose to respond to the negative aspect of not being able to enter Haiti by reframing the Dominican Republic stayover into a positive solution leading to a pathway for success. "This is yet another example of her indomitable spirit," Betsy explains and adds, "Our team of 13 people (including 3 doctors) was in Dominican Republic (DR), but we managed to arrange for bus transportation into Haiti so we could assist in relief efforts. Not knowing what to expect in Haiti, and how crazy things would be (very crazy it turns out), we thought it best that Mom remain in DR."

The group left Mother Kennedy with the Church Of God In Christ Dominican Republic Supervisor, Mother Mercedes Amancio. "By the time we returned six days later, Mom not only had the whole hotel staff wrapped around her finger, but she had also discovered a Haitian refugee community just a quarter of a mile or so from the hotel, and had started a school there for the children! The school is still going strong today, and we visit it every time we're in DR."

The next generation will face an increasingly complex world. Using the Kennedy's as a model for leadership in international missions, their love has flowed through their family's sacrifices causing hundreds of thousands of individuals to have hope. Undeniably, the authentic legacy of Father and Mother Kennedy is a legacy of love. Cuban Supervisor Madai

Haiti after the earthquake Reuters Photo.

Garcia says that their love shows action. Through Community of Caring, the Kennedy's team has provided medical and other supplies as well as financial support to Cuba in a time when it was problematic to do so. Arriving in Cuba for Convocation services, testament to Community of Caring's assistance is exhibited on a handmade poster showing images of the founder of the Church Of God In Christ, the founder of the Church Of God In Christ in Cuba, and Charles and Mary Beth Kennedy.

Bishop Matthews says that love flowed through their conversations on many subjects such as entomology, theology, psychology, musicology, super heroes, culinary advice, and history especially COGIC history.

The fact that Eld Kennedy was literally a rocket scientist made it fascinating. After late night conversations, Sharon and I would lie in bed all night processing what was discussed and dreaming further. His ability to share apologetics about Intelligent Design was unparalleled. I believe Elder Kennedy's last sermon was preached at my church. It was defense of the existence and power of God. He converted his walker into a chair and with dangling feet, this Giant of a man spoke with an unparalleled anointing. Further, he preached the most profound sermon on the Eucharist I have EVER heard at my dinner table. The sacrifice of Christ was so beautiful to him that he broke down weeping as he talked of it! I was encouraged to never "dumb down" the gospel but to preach where the people are and then take them where they need to be all in the same sermon. He preached with the belief that all people are anointed and intelligent....that's real love!!!

K

Five

Work On the Home Front

By the late 1950s American culture was on the cusp of change. In the middle 1950s Americans had jobs that paid well and were seemingly satisfied with life. The decade to follow brought hopes for a better tomorrow as the winds of change swept the nation. Children were taught middle class values that included believing in God, working hard and giving service to their country. Now new demands for equality rang out across the land and political action among students would come to an all-time high. During his presidential campaign in 1960, President John F. Kennedy promised an ambitious domestic agenda of laws and reforms that sought to eliminate injustice and inequality in the United States. To some the dreams of a nation died when President Kennedy was assassinated in Dallas, Texas November 22, 1963. Malaise would engulf the country as Civil Rights Leader Dr. Martin Luther King then Presidential Candidate Robert Kennedy were murdered. America's hope turned to anger and violence and increasingly riots seemed to be the rule of the day.

More Americans protested to demand an end to the unfair treatment of Black citizens. Others protested to demand an end to the war in Vietnam. Still others protested to demand full equality for women. In the midst of the national tumult, in Erie, Pennsylvania there were still needs to be met. The Kennedy's saw a need, prayed, and then put feet to their prayers.

The Kennedy's direct experience and knowledge of organizing and establishing institutions for learning would aid them in performing some impressive feats. They established four different schools: Lee Elementary and Wissikeh Academy in Liberia, West Africa, built while they were on the mission field were the only schools within a radius of 5 miles through the jungle. Finding themselves back in the United States after serving full time in the mission field at Wissikeh, the Kennedy's found a way to meet the needs of humanity on the home front.

Life lessons are not always taught but many times are demonstrated. Their offspring have direct knowledge and experience in the family business of missions and have been integral to the work. They honestly shared insight into what works for the children of missionaries. As a teen, daughter Betsey had vivid examples of serving as she observed her mother visiting bereaved individuals or ministering to those experiencing severe illness.

"As you can imagine, I was very bored with all those grown people, and had no desire to be there. When I questioned her on why I had to go, her response was that it was good training for me, and that I needed to learn to show compassion and do for others.

As the years passed, Betsy and her siblings would have ample opportunity to further evaluate what it meant to serve the Lord through serving humanity.

In 1968 the Community Country Day School (grades 1-8) and later the Community Preparatory Academy (grades 9-12) opened their doors to children who were labeled socially maladjusted and who needed a safe place to learn. "During the unrest of the 1960s," Mother Kennedy says, "more and more schools began to ostracize children because they 'couldn't handle' them." She used a $400 inheritance to give a love token to the bus driver, paid a cook and got started

establishing the Community Country Day School. The Catholic Benedictine Sisters of Erie lent them a crafts building where they held classes for a month. The school served students that no one else could handle as well as other students in grades 1-12. Vicki Stetson, one of CCDSs charter teachers, began in 1968 and was "totally unprepared. We held classes in an old farm house and the classes had hardly any books. Teachers were resigning because a teacher had been assaulted."

Staff and faculty alike diffused situations by giving the children unconditional love. The school's motto? *Love Can Change the World.* From the school's inception the guiding principles were integrity, relationships and hard work but it was the foundation of love that moved them forward. It was during its infancy that Mother Kennedy wrote *Love Therapy,* a major training tool for staff and instructors still in use today. Many CCDS students live in the inner city and the family profile (mostly single mothers and low income) destined them to fail. *Love Therapy* also encourages and teaches students to make right choices. The training teaches them to let the children—many who have behavioral and academic problems, struggle with drugs, attempted suicides, suffer because family members who should have cared for them were abusive – know that they all are God's children, that God loves them all, and He is always there for each of them. *Love Therapy* became the nucleus for a turning point in many of their lives. The concept uses interactions as a canvass to paint an umbrella for staff to overshadow all children with love, teach them and discipline them with love, so that no matter the environment of origin, they feel safe and wanted. This gives them an optimum chance for success.

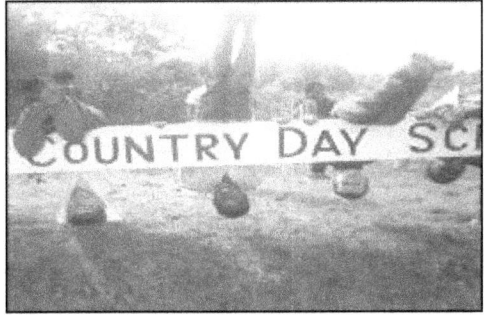

From the late 1960s until the 1980s Cynthia Manna spent her days off from work at her regular job as a second grade volunteer teacher's aide at the school which she says is "a sign of hope for every person in Erie." She was inspired by the school's reverence for life as they recognized the gifts of each person. "Whether those gifts are shining for all to see, or whether they are hidden by a shell of fear, defensively or resentment because of hurts, mistakes, and past bad choices.

Community Country Day School Theme Song

(Sung to the tune of "When the Saints Go Marching In")

Oh, we know love can change the world.
Oh, we know love can change the world.
It won't be quick, it won't be easy,
But we know love can change the world.

The love of God can change the world.
The love of God can change the world.
It won't be quick, it won't be easy,
But we know love can change the world.

There is hope for the community when such needs are recognized and addressed in a loving, caring and firm manner." She always taught her team to have faith in God. As a symbol of goodwill until times were better, the couple used personal funds to pay teacher salaries in lean times. On more than one occasion Manna marveled at Mother Kennedy's faith "whether we needed $1,000 or $10,000 she always said God will provide." Manna admitted that this would some of them crazy including one of the supporters, a CEO of a company, when she insisted in what may have seemed impractical "but she continued to tell us God WILL provide. And the next day the money came in the exact amount needed."

Whether taking a group of students to *Right to Life* marches or struggling to be recognized as a viable force within the community neither of the Kennedy's ever backed down from a fight. Currently, CCDS is a non-denominational private school, licensed Mental Health provider (Partial Hospitalization Program), and approved Private School for Emotional Disturbance. They also offer a Social Rehabilitation program. According to the Erie power structure, that portion of the school's profile was not to be. Karen Kitza, current principal of CCDS, met Mother Kennedy in 1980 when she interviewed for the position of high school English teacher.

She remembers the 1980s as a time when the school encountered serious challenges, prevailing against all odds. The school was notified it would not be licensed. Because of decreased funding the programs the school would be able to provide would be cancelled. They countered with a law suit. The case went from the preliminary through all courts up to and including the Pennsylvania Supreme Court.

"One of the major setbacks for the school was that the State of Pennsylvania did not want to recognize the school as a licensed Emotional Support school. The Kennedy's were not willing to back down to the several years and very public fight that would ensue as a result of not giving up. They had (and still have) a lawyer that was willing to be on the board and fight several legal battles that eventually resulted in the school becoming only one of two Approved Private Schools in Erie County. This allows the school to service and be paid for the work they were already doing with some of the Emotionally Disturbed children. There was a celebratory dinner that I remember attending after a few years of working here. It united staff to continue serving God and this population knowing that the efforts were now being recognized by the Department of Education."

Kitza recalls one incident in which Kennedy's *Love Therapy* discipline demonstrated how even the "scariest" child could be changed by God's love.

Give me the knife, [Mrs. Kennedy] spoke quietly but firmly never moving her eyes from the slim six-foot student towering over her.

Mrs. Kennedy, some of them said they're going to jump us. The "them" referred to a half-dozen African-American students.

You know we don't allow you to take matters into your own hands here. We'll take care of it. Please give me the knife.

I need it to open boxes at work.

Give me the knife, Jackson.

Slowly he took the ten-inch hunting knife from its sheath and handed the razor sharp instrument to her.

You may go to your next class.

Mrs. Kennedy and those trained in *Love Therapy* feel that when used in classroom management

1. the classroom becomes a much more humane place, the uptight atmosphere that often exists in many schools disappears between student and teachers alike

2. Disciplines prevails. Although teachers and students are friendly they are not buddies.

3. There is no fear on the part of teachers or students.

4. Learning takes place.

Their old African mission's mentor, Martha Barber, was one of the first commencement speakers. As a result of the school's success in positive behavior patterns and increased academic scores, the Country Day School became famous. Money was donated and they purchased nineteen acres to build a new facility in Erie's more pastoral area.

In the school's 55 year history they have done may things right and it has grown. The library is state of the art; the school has a huge regulation gymnasium, a computer center and classrooms, which serve grades 1 through 12. Some graduates — physicians, businesspersons, good citizens — believe they are doing well because of "Mrs. Kennedy's School." Rahshee Harris, now a successful independent contractor self-identifies himself as "a troubled youth" and reported he experienced unconditional love at the school. "I was kicked out of two middle schools, three high schools and then we heard about CCDS. Although it was a private school and costs money, they didn't hound me after I enrolled. We felt loved even if only [during] the day. They showed us how to give love...it made me care more about people and I changed. I even won awards for *Best Smile, Most Likely to*

Succeed, Sportsmanship, and others."

The Kennedys excelled in each of their complementary leadership roles. Now, the legacy of stewardship in educating the next generation continues under the direction of the detailed guidance of Aaron and the gregarious and outgoing Angela Collins. Aaron, a former Canadian Football League player is the grandson-in-law to Mother Kennedy. During a time that interest waned in moving forward in educating inner city youth, it was through Aaron's insight in the vital importance of the institution to the targeted populace that brought Mother Kennedy's granddaughter Angela back to Erie and her legacy as the Executive Director of the Community Country Day School. Says Aaron, "Mother Kennedy stands alone as a trailblazer. Other people have started schools, others are missionaries, and others have opened shelters, and worked with orphans. Others have done great works too. But I've not met one person who could not identify with the difference her agencies embody. The peace associated with her great work. She fosters the atmosphere of love."

Angie always knew that her grandparents were special and adds "It was hard not to know because everywhere we went we would hear that. They were instrumental in changing so many lives and establishing works that will live on." One of those works is the Community Country Day School.

The Collins', parents of four boys, understand that every child does not have a positive home environment but each child has to be loved. And their work embodies the school's underlying principle that *Love Can Change the World.* As administrators they are committed to educating the child: academically, physically, emotionally and socially. Currently the school provides state-licensed educational and mental health programs as an alternative to costly inpatient psychiatric care for children and adolescents.

While Mother Kennedy is out of the day-to-day school management her faith coupled with her savvy business experience continues to aid the operations. "Approximately two years ago," Angie explained, "the financial situation at the school was getting hard. The school district wasn't paying their portion, donors were down and major funding sources were drying up. It was at this time my husband and I were able to see her extreme faith, strength and sheer resolve to not allow the dream to die. Even at the age of 86 she dug her heels in and coupled her prayers with action. She is a fund raiser like no other!! She knew how to ask even when it was EXTREMELY uncomfortable. I had heard her say that someone years prior had brought payroll to her door in a paper bag full of exactly the right amount of cash. My husband and I learned so much from her through this time. "

The couple has learned to continue to have faith and with 17 teachers and counselors the Collins' follow the legacy of providing a loving and accepting educational environment for every student. Since that trying time their philosophy has renewed interest in the school and community leaders such as those from the Erie Community Foundation have taken note and granted substantial donations.

The original vision of the founders continues as regular education students and partial hospitalization program students learn in the intentional small class size environment. With success stories from former students such as one Erie Firefighter who came to the school as a troubled third grader continue to be told, it has caused the school to have a growing waiting list.

K

Six

Community of Caring and Dayenu

When the Kennedy's started out on their adventure of mission and mercy, they likely had no idea the powerful impact their leadership would have on their family and the world. Winning, nurturing and developing souls moved the Kennedys forward in unusual but practical ways in over 50 years of service. Father Kennedy was an ordained elder in the Church Of God In Christ and founded the House of Prayer Church Of God In Christ. Seeing the need for continued humanitarian activities they set out to provide international and stateside provisions through the Community Drop in Shelter (1973), through Erie's first emergency counseling facility for runaways, addicts, alcoholics and people having suicidal tendencies (now Community Shelter

Services) and Community of Caring (1980), a social service agency that concentrates on helping the "newly poor" and chronically unemployed by providing the basic necessities of life, including food, shelter and counseling.

In the 1960s the population of Erie increased to 138,440. As the City of Erie's homeless population increased the Kennedy's noticed that there was not a facility to serve that demographic. As a result they set out to and established drop in shelters where the homeless slept, get a cup of coffee and be provided with something warm to eat. Their forward thinking was noted by the United Way and that agency took over the Community Shelter Services. To show the high esteem in which they hold her, the agency honored Mother Kennedy by hanging a large portrait of her in the building.

Twice a week COC provides meals to 50-60 homeless children ranging from ages 4-12. They share the meals with the children which consists of nshema (yellow meal) and greens with a bit of fish. As director, Mother Kennedy had the responsibility for oversight of the residential transition facility where assistance and daily meals are provided. Their former church was transformed into one of several facilities scattered throughout the city where vulnerable populations are served through residential programs, hot meal programs and transitional housing. The County and State provide funding through the agency's 501c3 status.

After completing a robust certificate process, COC was registered with the U.S. Agency for International Development as a Private Voluntary Organization (PVO). Community of Caring International is active in a number of states as well as Cuba, Haiti, Tanzania and Liberia. Each year shipments sent to one or two countries are valued at $50,000 - $60,000. COC collects huge truckloads of food, clothing, medicine and other relief supplies for its international affiliates in Tanzania, Liberia, Sierra Leone, Ghana, Democratic Republic of Congo and Zambia.

The country of Cuba is one of the recipients of the COC resources. It is less than 100 miles off the coast of Florida but until recently had no official relationship. The Church Of God In Christ in Cuba was born in 1947 after being prayed out by Pastor Guillermini Ugarte after she was introduced to the movement by saints in Colombia. She brought the word to Pastor (later Bishop) Wilfredo Garcia who built the first Church Of God In Christ in Cuba. After the Cuban Revolution, on January 1, 1959 when Fidel Castro seized power from President Fulgencio Batista relations between the United States and Cuba deteriorated resulting in a break of relations in 1961 and the church began to operate under pressure. (The Neftali Church Of God In Christ Theological Seminary of Cuba has clandestinely held classes over 40 years and would not give up its desire to stay true to the doctrine and its heritage since Bishop Garcia established the first church.) Bishop Carlis Moody, Bishop P.A. Brooks and others made trips to encourage the work during the tense relations between the two countries. Currently the Jurisdictional Prelate of Cuba, Bishop Jose Mesa Videaux and Mother Madai Garcia, the Supervisor of the Department of Women carry on the work.

Through an interpreter Garcia explained "the Kennedy's were the founders of the [Cuban branch of] Community of Caring in 1987 which started in a field behind the church. They brought medicine, food and clothing. After church the older saints would come out back where coffee and cassava were shared as seedlings for the feeding project. Since 2004, through the Cuban COC, seventy adults and one hundred children are fed three days per week." The pair have visited Cuba many times since 1987 taking a plane into Mexico then over to the Dominican Republic or one of the islands to enter. While there they encouraged the Cubans and also taught the basic doctrine of the COGIC. "The fruit in Cuba has grown because of the seed they planted."

Haiti, the world's first postcolonial Black republic and the second country to gain independence (in 1804), was the

most popular destination for American Blacks. Under the leadership of François Dominique Toussaint L'Ouverture and second in command Jean-Jaques Dessalines, both ex-slaves, 40,000 of the French colony's 465,429 slaves revolted.[17] Since its nationhood this Caribbean country of 10 million has had its share of ill fortune as the 20th century brought three decades of American occupation, multiple corrupt regimes, natural disasters, environmental devastation, and in more recent history, the scourge of HIV. The country is another example of the service COC provides throughout the global community. Since a major earthquake struck on January 12, 2010 there has been a tremendous outpour of support. But the Kennedy's COC has had a presence in the country for many years.

In 1983 the Kennedy's led a team to Haiti carrying with 600

---

[17] Robinson, Randall, *Haiti: The Truth African-Americans Have Not Been Allowed to Know,* Ebony Magazine, April 2010, 78-79

pounds of medicines, food and clothing. It was important for the team to let the people know who they were as ambassadors sent from God who would heal them and who had provided provision. "We held three clinics sessions and did laboratory screening for intestinal parasites on all of the children of the orphanage," Mother Kennedy. The first was in Port Au Prince, the second in the county town called Petit Gouave and the last in Bel Aire at the Church Of God In Christ[18]," she recalled.

The team, led by Father and Mother Kennedy treated malaria, arthritis, malnutrition, generalized weakness, cough, colds, prenatal difficulties, hypertension, intestinal parasites, and other diseases. "We told the people that all healing really came from God and everything we did was to be for His glory."

The political crisis stemming from its disputed election in 2000 continued to negatively impact Haitians in 2003. Haitians

---

[18] Williams Goodson, Glenda, *Royalty Unveiled Lancaster:* HCM Publishing, 150, 153 (Bel Aire is the Mother Church of Haiti. Elder Joseph Paulceus, a Haitian brother who lived in the U.S.A. was saved in the Church Of God In Christ in the early 1920's as the evangelist Annie Pennington—later Mother Annie Bailey—preached sanctification and Holy Ghost Baptism on the streets. In the spring of 1928 he felt led of the Lord to go back to Haiti, his homeland, to preach to his people the Gospel of Jesus Christ, according to the patterns set in the Acts of the Apostles. He went to Bishop C.H. Mason who prayed for him, gave him a tent, enough funds for his voyage and he boarded a boat for Haiti. He arrived in Port-au-Prince, the capital of that country on July 2, 1928. In January 1929, they held the first service of the Church Of God In Christ in Haiti. Later the Church was moved to Bel 'air where the tent given by Bishop Mason was fixed. Meanwhile, Brother St. Juste continued to pay the rent for this property until 1947 when it was bought for the church by Bishop and Sister C.H. Mason and Mother Coffey.)

struggled to make ends meet following a 60% depreciation of the national currency (gourde) between September 2002 and March 2003 and a 35–45% annual inflation rate during much of the year.[19] From a report to the Church Of God In Christ Department of Women General Supervisor Willie Mae Rivers, Mother Kennedy reported:

In January 2003 COC visited the country where raw sewage runs through ditches separating the buildings. Approximately 100,000 persons are crammed together in conditions of unbelievable poverty. They completed a clinic session in Cite Solcil, perhaps the worst slums in the Western Hemisphere where thousands of makeshift one room shacks two or three feet apart stretch as far as the eye can see. Into this area we came, a dozen American missionaries offered medical up work stations; two nurses took blood pressures; three did patient consultants; two helped out licensed pharmacist set out medications, one screened for exophthalmia, two went up to the second floor (where there was adequate light) to check eyes and dispense glasses, and one floated. Hour after hour they dispensed large quantities of pharmaceutical supplies to individuals with coughs, colds, hypertension, anemia, malnutrition, malaria, intestinal diseases, parasites and xerophthalmia, one of the leading cause of blindness in Third World countries, caused be a severe Vitamin A deficiency.

[19] http://www.britannica.com/EBchecked/topic/917029/Haiti-in-2003

They faced dangers but their perception of the enemy's power never overshadowed their confidence in God. More than once their confidence and self-possession caused them to provide resources despite the danger. Once a half-dozen, tough-looking young men entered pushing their way through to the front of the consultation line and faced the very definition of cohesion and discipline: The team continued working rapidly, efficiently and in an orderly manner with no outward show of fear. They gave vitamins to everyone, even some to those who were threatening them. "I believe that this God-directed spontaneous act of kindness to our enemies, who would harm us, confused them and gave us the opportunity to escape."

To get things done the humanitarians knew and utilized the value of partnerships. Community of Caring organized Project Hunger to aid relief efforts in the Njombe District of Tanzania, East Africa. By 1990, 62 year old Tony Manna was inspired to accept the challenge to raise funds and supplies. "The primary recipient of Project Hunger [was] the Njombe District Development Trust, a group that supplies various schools and hospitals. Also included are two interior missions and Tanzania's only school for the deaf." During the time of severe drought and famine over six years the Project provided rice, beans, medical supplies and peanut butter.

As crises occur with growing rapidity and international commitment erodes as resources are diverted, the work started by the Kennedys continues. And it is very important for partnerships and alliances to continue successfully. Keenly aware that COC needed as seamless a transition of leadership as possible to successfully provide services in the future, the Kennedys initiated succession planning.

Some organizations set up formal transfers of leadership to occur *after* their death however, after 50 years of shouldering the brunt of the work associated with caring for so many needs around the world the day to day operation of organizing and supplying resources has been transferred to Dr. Grace Kennedy, the youngest of the Kennedy clan. The Director of Development and International Medical Director left her medical practice to work to help heal the hurting poor. This strategic move, to allow the younger generation to be guided and supported by an alert and experienced older generation, permitted a significant amount of experience and learning of leadership responsibilities to be passed to the next generation.

This was a plus as a shared vision for the future could be assured. As of this writing, the current leadership is listed below:

Board of Directors

COC also partners with Sight and Life, an organization with headquarters in Basel, Switzerland, dedicated to the eradication of exophthalmia, the leading cause of blindness in Third World countries. "Massive doses (200,000 I.U.) of Vitamin A can prevent and/or treat this condition. During Mission Of Mercy, we usually conduct screenings and administer the Vitamin A capsules. We did this at Kinshasa Community Of Caring Center."

Dayenu House
(Multigenerational Support/Community Center)

Something unusual happened when a couple wished to simply be faithful in helping humanity in whatever way the Lord would see fit. They found that provision is made for vision and God could do exceedingly and abundantly more than they could ever imagine. And He is to be praised. In the Jewish Celebration of Passover a song recalling the historical evidence for His redemption from Egyptian slavery up to the building of the Temple is sung to praise His faithfulness. This is Dayenu, some of which is recorded below:

How many levels of favors has the Omnipresent One bestowed upon us:

If He had brought us out from Egypt, and had not carried out judgments against them--Dayenu, it would have sufficed us!

If He had split the sea for us, and had not taken us through it on dry land--Dayenu, it would have sufficed us!

If He had taken us through the sea on dry land, and had not drowned our oppressors in it--Dayenu, it would have sufficed us!

If He had drowned our oppressors in it, and had not supplied our needs in the desert for 40 years--Dayenu, it would have sufficed us!

If He had supplied our needs in the desert for 40 years, and had not fed us the manna--Dayenu, it would have sufficed us!

If He had brought us into the land of Israel, and had not built for us the Beit Habechirah (Chosen House; the Beit Hamikdash)--Dayenu, it would have sufficed us!

The essence of this song is "if God doesn't do anything else, He's done enough...*to praise Him!*" In every step of the missionary life observed through the Kennedy's, God has been faithful. Although Father Kennedy is now present with the Lord, Mother Kennedy continues the couple's legacy of service to humanity a piece of hope called the *Dayenu House,* a relatively new addition to the family of caring.

The Center, a modern, brightly lit and airy facility, was built from the ground up with funds donated by one of Erie's wealthiest citizens who honors Mother Kennedy's community work. At *Dayenu House* everyone is welcome, from those just needing a weekly meal to others who want a second chance and new start. Rodney Walker is an example of a recipient who has come back to volunteer. He accompanies Mother

Kennedy to churches where she explains the work that she does and has also visited area television stations where she appears. He remembers that "Father Kennedy was a godly man and [I am happy to continue] working with Mother Kennedy." The staff at *Dayenu House* feeds the elderly and Rodney says, "anyone who comes a free weekly family Sunday dinner."

Each first Thursday it's time for *Share the Spirit*, a monthly luncheon where diverse and intergenerational members of the community gather to have lunch and talk about spiritual things. At *Dayenu House* the staff does as best they can to respond to those whose spirits have faltered. On any given day a local television reporter may pop in to hear the latest news of COC or the Center and they are refreshed, or those who are emotionally damaged are affirmed by a passing kind word.

K

Seven

Into the Everywhere

Understanding the significance of connections within the framework of her denomination and realizing the influence she could wield using soft diplomacy in a real word of limited funds, the savvy Mother Kennedy accepted the position as Supervisor of the Democratic Republic of Congo (DRC), the second largest country on the continent of Africa. The Church Of God In Christ was established in eastern the part of the country (then known as Zaire) in Lubumbashi following a revival by Bishop Maimela from Botswana. DRC covers about 905,000 square miles and has a population of 63 million people. The country is widely considered to be the richest country in the world regarding natural resources, with untapped deposits of raw minerals estimated to be worth in excess of $24 trillion (USD). Congo is much more jungle with gigantic hardwoods soaring to heights of 170 feet. "You walk through that canopy and it's so beautiful and you just think about the majesty of God," Mother Kennedy recalled.

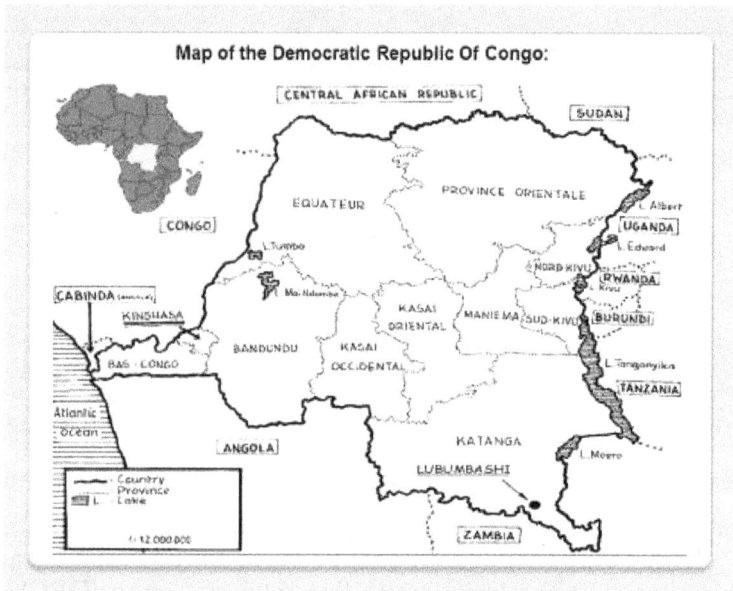

Map courtesy of Sandra Wright

Despite the potential wealth of the country, by contrast seventy one percent of the population lives below the poverty line. Mother Kennedy remembered

One time we were riding around down in the Congo to go to one of the meetings and I looked because some of them were standing down by the edge of the road at one of the market places. And it looked like

there were rats in her hand. And I said to someone in the car, I said those look like rats. She had four of them; she was holding them by their tails hanging down. And they said they are. And they were selling them for dinner.

Since 1996, the DRC has been involved in what has been called the African World War with over 5.4 million killed. A peace accord in 2003 was to have ended the vicious civil war, however, armed conflict has continued in pockets of the country, especially in the east. Despite the countries large quantities of gold, copper, diamonds, and coltan (a mineral used in cell phones), severe poverty, insecurity, lack of basic social services and sexual violence (rape used as a weapon of war) all continue to take a heavy toll on its citizens, especially children.[20]

Most people do not have jobs. Many of those who do work for the mines and mine laborers earn from $10 to $20 per month. A person earning $15 per month might buy a 100 lb. stack of cornmeal (white cornmeal, lacking in nutrition - no yellow available on the market) and a few bunches of greens, which could feed his family of 10 or 12 one meal every other day for a month. That amount of money ($15) could also buy 10 lbs. of

---

[20] http://www.unicef.org/wcaro/Countries_1749.html

rice, 10 dried fish, 2 avocados, 8 bananas, 2 bunches of greens, 1 bunch of onions: for one good nutritious meal that would feed his family for one day. Needless to say, millions eat the cheap but filling cornmeal mush and don't even get that on a daily basis. If families eat one meal a day, they consider themselves fortunate. Many eat only two or three meals a week. Nor are their meals nutritious and representative of all the major food groups. Usually the meal consists of nshema, which is a stiff cornmeal mush and few vegetables cooked in a stew. Rarely is there meat or fish. There is simply no money for a more nutritious diet.

Most of the Congolese live in crowded conditions of almost unbelievable poverty and squalor. Because of the civil war, many children live in the streets and field like animals, eating garbage, rats, worms and anything else to try to keep alive.

This is particularly sad because the climate permits a year-around-growing season. Fresh fruits and vegetables abound: oranges, bananas, plantains, papaya, mangoes, sweet potatoes, cabbage, onions, various types of leafy greens, etc. The problem is that everything is very expensive, priced well beyond what a typical family can afford.

In the midst of all that is happening in the country God is accomplishing the impossible, especially through the Church

Of God In Christ where Bishop Gabriel Hichika Mayuke is Jurisdictional Bishop. Bishop Mayuke started with his own family in the 1970's. He now has 115 churches in an area of about 250,000 square miles. While Mother Kennedy is away from DRC Mother Godalieve Mayuke oversees the bands and auxiliaries which are very active throughout the region for the destitute children who are suffering and dying.

Although she has not lived in DRC as she did in Liberia for seven years, she and Father Kennedy made many short term mission trips to the country. She has also sent international missionaries Marva Nyema and Betty Gardner Harris to serve the people and represent the Church.

The Antioch Church Of God In Christ took the initiative and provided most of the funds for two Church Of God In Christ orphanages in the DRC. The Church Of God In Christ Orphanage in Lubumbashi in the southeastern part of the country is the first official Church Of God In Christ Orphanage built on the continent of Africa houses seventy-nine children. Almost all of those children were orphaned because of the war, AIDS, malaria or other tropical maladies. "They are so pitiful, terribly thin and malnourished, many ill from various diseases. Some of them have watched their parents die and are suffering severe emotional problems. They

are finding food, health treatment, education and God's love and grace in their new home in the Lubumbashi orphanage." A second orphanage has been built for these wretched, homeless, abandoned children. They were extremely malnourished and actually dying of starvation. Many lives had been saved through the feeding program. Even though the orphanage is now functioning, there are many more needy children than the orphanage can serve. These children receive food (usually only a bowl of cornmeal mush and a few vegetables) two or three times a week. It is barely enough to keep them alive but they are very grateful. The director of the center and the fledgling Church Of God In Christ at Famalu Area, Kinshasa is Bishop Fabrice Malundama Mbumba. Primary school classes are given although as yet there is no school building. A rudimentary medical center is also in place. Another bright spot in the country is the construction of the first Church Of God In Christ hospital in the world, built by Bishop Mbumba. Bishop Mbumba is also The Kinshasa Community of Caring Branch Director, which was very helpful in 2001 during a precarious situation when the Kennedys and Elder Havious Green (the American side of the Mission of Mercy Team) ran into difficulties in DRC. Getting to Democratic Republic of Congo is difficult and takes several days. The group was routed through Rome, Italy and Johannesburg, South Africa and then flew into Kinshasa, the capital of DRC for a 3-hour layover before going on to their final destination, Lubumbashi. Mother Kennedy recalls, "We waited. Everyone else in the terminal left to get on the plane. We were told that it was not our plane. Naturally, they had our passports....déjà vu. We inquired as to when we might go. We were told 'Sorry, but your plane has been cancelled. You cannot go'." It was one thing to observe how power works in a country but another to maneuver through the details. That's where the couple's strategy of having national partners on the ground came in handy. Mbumba's family, with a sophisticated understanding of the government, came to the rescue by using their influence to negotiate the return of their passports.

Recollections from the Democratic Republic of Congo

The Kennedy's have never been ones who were afraid to lead and have operated as both training and sending agencies. They trained those with the heart for international missions and accompanied or sent them out to the Ivory Coast, to Ghana's Liberian refugee camps, Haiti, Cuba, Russia, The Dominican Republic, other African countries and finally The Democratic Republic of Congo. They have been a source of great inspiration as they partner with nationals who serve in their own countries.

Following are recollections (verbatim) from individuals who have accompanied the Kennedys, have been supported by the Kennedys or partner with them as they minister around the world.

Beginning far left, Pastor Derrick Anderson, Great Lakes Second Jurisdictional Missions President, Bishop and Mother Mauke, Tetaka (the cook).
Photo courtesy Evangelist Sandra Wright

Bishop Gabriel Hichika Mayuke is the Jurisdictional Prelate of the Democratic Republic of Congo. Along with his wife, Mother Godelive Chawa Itakika, the Church Of God In Christ is represented in the country with approximately 115 churches.

KENNEDYS: MISSIONARIES WITH GREAT VISION

I met Elder and Mother Kennedy in Memphis at the Church Of God In Christ Holy Convocation in 1995. They were very effective missionaries for many years in Africa. As first missionaries, they visited the Democratic Republic of Congo for the first time in 1996 with an evangelistic vision; to win souls for Christ (Matthew 25:35-36). Through prayers, the Word of God, many people joined the COGIC. The Kennedys used to feed and clothe the needy. Caring for them through their clinic.

The saints, Mother Mayuke and myself saw the love of Christ, joy and peace of God through the Kennedys. They suffered many things such as malaria and war. They were most fortunate persons on earth. They fed the hungry and starving orphans they took care of sick people. Missionaries with great vision, they project to build orphanages in every Jurisdiction.

They preferred to eat shima; cassava leaves etc. They socialized with all people, they stimulated other Missionaries to come to Congo. I have realised that they were strong people in Congo within the Church Of God In Christ. Mother Mary Beth Kennedy is a leader (Supervisor to the Congo). She taught the Sunshine Band (children's ages 5 to 12). She organized the Sewing Circle, women's conferences up to now. She assists with the work in Congo in so many ways!

Pastor Hitshika Ghilain is the son of Bishop Gabriel Hichika Mayuke, the Jurisdictional Prelate of the Democratic Republic of Congo. He works with his father distributing funds to the orphanages.

I will tell you what I know about the Kennedys, their history and work in Africa and The Democratic Republic of Congo in particular.

Bishop Mayuke made a trip to the United States of America by the will of God. The Spirit of the Lord directed him to get

get acquainted with Mother Mary Beth Kennedy and Elder Charles Kennedy. Afterwards, Bishop Mayuke invited them to visit the Congo. In 1996 Dad Kennedy and Mother Kennedy arrived in the Congo by way of Zambia. This was both her and her husband's first missionary trip to the Congo. They have done much work in the Congo. The fruit of their labor remains until this day.

He taught doctrine, conducted Bible studies and supported pastors to Congolese pastors, elders and deacons from different parishes and districts. They evangelized most of the District of Congo, Kinshasa District, District of Kolwezi, District Kipushi, District Kasumbalesa and the District of Likasi.

Mother Kennedy is the President National Women's Department of the Congo (Supervisor), it was she who initiated and organized the Women's Conventions in the Congo which are held annually in July. Mother Mary worked in collaboration with Mother Mayuke who oversees the work of mothers in the Congo.

Mother and Dad Kennedy also supervised the Sunday School for the children, giving food and medicine. They also started three orphanages in Kinshasa, Lubumbashi and Kolwezi

Pastor Derrick Anderson, State Missions President, Great Lake Jurisdiction, ministering the gospel with Pastor Robert (interpreter). The major languages are French and Swahili.
Photo courtesy of Sandra Wright

District. Mother and Dad Kennedy brought other missionaries to the Congo. Pastor Derrick Anderson, Missionary Sandra Wright and others stayed with us. They are still working today for Congo sending support for the Orphanage in the Kolwezi District (Bishop Mayuke's childhood home). Mother and Dad Kennedy have marked the history of the Congo church. She has the ministry of love, courage, sacrifice and dedication. My prayer is that God would continue to bless her.

Pastor Ghilain

Missionary Sandra Wright with Orphans at COGIC Orphanages in Kolwezi
Photo Courtesy of Sandra Wright

Missionary Sandra Wright is a member of Antioch Church Of God In Christ. Her pastor Elder Derrick Anderson is the State Missions President and her jurisdiction (Bishop Alfred Smith, Jurisdictional Prelate Great Lakes Jurisdiction) are strong missions supporters. For over 12 years Great Lakes and Antioch has sent a sizable monthly stipend to the DRC. Following are her recollections of one of her trips with the Kennedys.

Thanks to Mother Kennedy I had a story to share with our Jurisdiction from my second trip in 2007: We woke at 5am. Did not want to miss prayer. We thought we would be praying with Bishop Mayuke and the some of the members of the family and church. They had already prayed at 5am. We were not aware that the people leave so early for work (early to rise and early to bed). So the team prayed outside in the

Bishop's church (still under construction, as with many other building projects in Congo). After prayer we had tea, coffee, one egg and some bread. That was our daily breakfast menu, normally the people eat only once a day. This was only possible because the team bought our own food while there.

After breakfast we went shopping with Mother Mayuke, (Bishop's wife), to buy food for two orphanages, one in Lubumbashi and the Mary J in Kowelzi, the house and the team. We went so many places and experienced so many problems with the money exchange. There were many money-exchangers that sat outside on the side-walks of most marketplaces and exchanged money right there on the spot. The Congolese people are very particular about the money they accept. We were unable to exchange several $100, $20.00 and especially $1.00 bills. The money cannot have even the slightest rip or tear or it will not be accepted. But the irony of it all was that the Francs (French money), was so filthy that it was amazing that they would even consider refusing our crisp $100.00 bills fresh from the US banks.

We arrived at the orphanage in Lubumbashi. We presented the children with toys and school supplies that we had brought with us from home. Each team member packs a separate suitcase just to transport whatever items we will be taking for that trip due to the fact that the cost to send anything over is astronomical. Our translator, Robert Kauya gave us a tour of the orphanage. While we were walking we saw the women preparing the food for the children. The mama's (cooks), asked us if we could help by buying a large stick that they could use to stir the pot. Apparently it was too expensive for them to purchase. As it turned out the stick cost only $5.00 (US). We gladly gave them money to buy the stick. They were so happy for such a small request was granted.

The children eat once per day (maybe), a meal consisting of shima (boiled cornmeal mush), smoked fish (very rarely), and some type of red sauce. They had a huge pot that they cook in over hot coals. They stir the cornmeal until it is very still then they pile it out with a small bowl and put it on the plates for the children. Some of the children sit on the floor (in the midst of chicken poop and dirt), others on benches at make-shift tables (Deb cried when she saw how the children had to eat). They take a portion of the meal, dip it in the sauce and eat with their little dirty fingers. There is no water and the electricity is patchy, at best. While touring the orphanage we were asked to pray for a little girl, named Abigail, who was sick with fever (malaria). Deb and I prayed for her (the next day we were told that she was up and running about as if she never had a fever). We continued on thru the orphanage. We took pictures of the bathrooms for the girls and boys. They were in horrible condition. It was unthinkable that any child would have to suffer such conditions and on an everyday basis.

Of all of the toys were distributed (mostly puzzles, pencil boxes, books, little hand-held toys, the puzzles seemed to have been the most popular). They were Blues-Clues puzzles. The sad thing is that they children, never having had many toys, did not even know how to put the puzzles together. They had turned the base up-side down and was building the puzzle on the back of the package. We are so blessed in the US. Our children would frown at such simple gifts and complain that we spent very little money on them. These children curtsied and said thank-you when we gave them the toys. We also left medical supplies, mostly vitamins, antacids and skin creams with the orphanage director. Thanks to the concern of just a few people here, especially Linda Kirkwood-Brown, a member of our mission's team, the children had medical supplies that would hopefully last about 6 months. The only thing the director feared was that the vitamins encouraged healthy appetites but they had very little food to satisfy the renewed hunger.

The staff at the orphanage asked us to come back and ask our contributors to help purchase large barrels (for water), the huge pots for cooking, they need a refrigerator and an iron.

.

K

Eight

Her Children. . .Call Her Blessed

The impact missionaries such as the Kennedy's had on hundreds and thousands of individuals will only be fully revealed in glory. The divine imperative, which allowed them to do what seemed impossible, flowed from their faith in God and faithfulness to their assignment. Gazing into the future to a time when they were gone, they tasked their biological and spiritual offspring with responsibilities to carry on the work. The following have had the benefit of this remarkable couple's counsel as they too, take responsibility for serving "the least of these."

To longtime mission supporters Pastor Thomas Eagleton and

his wife Georgia the counsel from the Kennedy's have proved invaluable and they are encouraged to continue the cause of mission through their support. Their Crosby, Texas congregation has hosted the Kennedy's many times after their initial meeting in Indiana. "The Lord said to me to take $1,000.00 and when I got there I attended the Department of Missions services," Pastor Eagleton recalls. The Lord said 'give it here' and I asked Him who could I give the money to and...I spoke with Bishop Moody who introduced me to Mother Kennedy."

That meeting began a forever friendship that extends to family members, such as their nephew Kwame Eagleton, who traveled with the missionaries to Liberia. The Eagleton's agree that the fragrance of the lives of the "giant of a man" and his wife "touches all of our hearts. I am a recipient of the grace of God through the Kennedys," he said with his wife adding, "Mother Kennedy's words were life changing." In the late 1990s, this couple, with a heart for missions, questioned how missions funds were disbursed along with other disparities. They considered doing something "other than COGIC." Father Kennedy was small in stature but his words yet resonate with Mother Eagleton who sums their counsel by saying, "This exceptionally intelligent man could easily be overlooked until he opened his mouth and shared powerfully with us with wisdom and humor, while Mother Kennedy told us that the assignment was greater than feelings." They were the glue that helped to keep the church within the COGIC alliance. As late as 2007 Mother Kennedy visited their Crosby church where they held a dinner in her honor. She was a special delight to the children of the church and could recall many of them by name (the Eagleton's pastor a church with large congregation). She taught the children songs in English and Swahili dialects and displayed many artifacts from countries where they served.

Bishop Girardeau Nesbitt of Florida has accompanied the couple on many missions. "A few years ago I went into Wissikeh and it took eighteen hours to get there by plane. When the Kennedy's went into Liberia it took them 39 days traveling by ocean and land. It took me a week to get to Wissikeh traveling on a small path. When the Kennedy's came they had to actually beat and cut out a path." Evangelist Betty Gardner Harris has traveled to many countries with the Kennedy's. "I've seen her carry backpacks as we traveled through Liberia through the bush...even when her heart bothered her. I've been with her when we didn't have the proper food. She is Mrs. Missions." As she traveled, one of Mother Kennedy's gravest concerns was the safety of those who accompanied her. "There were some places that you'd never want to go." Bishop Girardeau Nesbitt waited one night in Kinshasha with Bishop Vincent Matthews until his visa was delivered. They sought a bus but it became mired in the mud and the two set out to walk miles to Kai City in the black dark. Darkness has its own perils and the two were vulnerable to thieves who preyed on travelers. "No lights," Betty Harris remembered, "and Mother Kennedy was very worried." Bishop Nesbitt recalled, "We saw someone from the United Nations who had a truck and offered to take us. Then he had a flat tire with no spare!" Much to the relief of their team the two made it safely to Kai City.

Charles and Mary Beth Kennedy's reach extends to service to humanity by children, grandchildren and spiritual children they have nurtured in over 50 years of ministry. Liberian national Jane Jabbeh is the wife of Benjamin Jabbeh, the first student to graduate from the Kennedy's Lee High School in Wissikeh. "Pa went to Wissikeh, perhaps fearful, but he went," she reported. "Mother Kennedy lived her life on the mission field. As late as the early 1990s Jane recalls the Kennedy's journeying to Africa and, because they found it unacceptable that children were dying, they would pray. However, they would also make sure agencies tasked to help would be the catalyst to answer those prayers. The crisis was so acute that the people ate leaves. "During 1990, 1992 we were hungry," Jane remembered, "No food. We lived on leaves. Stomach getting big. God sent Mother Kennedy. A little boy was crying and wanted food. Mother Kennedy prepared cabbage but he died before it was ready. The children began to steal. Some people practice other things. Mother Kennedy pray to God. She went into the bush. We protect ourself under the blood of Jesus. Mother Kennedy felt the people. She talked with organization and they established a feeding center. The children began to live. Through them people are still living in Liberia. Now her children are a root that is carrying on."

Emotionally and intellectually, the Kennedy offspring's upbringing has been of great help in continuing the legacy. Their oldest son, the late Charles Kennedy, Jr., and his wife, Cindy journeyed to Lexington, Mississippi where he taught at the Church Of God In Christ School under the leadership of Dr. Arenia Mallory. Cindy, who is Caucasian, remembers that during the turbulent 1960s it was dangerous for races to mix with the powers in Mississippi and other states without intention of ceding authority over the lives of those without power. But they were physically unharmed and extended their love and learning to the children of the saints and those in communities surrounding Lexington.

In the 1970s Charles and Cindy heard God's call to Belize, Central America. Cindy reported "after Elder and Mother Kennedy returned from the Church Of God In Christ Holy Convocation, they told us Bishop Bennett wanted someone to come and set up a high school...after much prayer we ended up in Belize" with their oldest child, Jennifer, still a nursing infant and Cindy pregnant with their second child (Angela, who was born in Belize). They served in that country for two years prior to returning to America. Prior to his untimely death Charles, a self-identified griot and noted flute player, would minister to people as he said "as my parents have done for more than 50 years. I may be doing it is a slightly different way, but I'm doing it."

FROM MARY (Oldest daughter): This is some of what I learned from my parents:
--Creativity
--Resourcefulness (making use of what's available; as Mom's mother used to say, "Taking what you have to make what you want.")
--Tenacity, a.k.a. stubbornness
--Deep loyalty to family

Near the end of my dad's life, I saw very clearly just how very close they were to each other. After he passed, and then when

Charles passed a few years later, I saw Mom leaning on the Lord as never before. I learned from both of my parents that a person's race, or color, truly does not matter. What is inside is FAR more important than what is outside. I can't speak for anyone else in the family, but I am grateful that I never went through an "identity crisis" with regards to race. What race am I? Human.

I've also begun to realize that my parents would have probably been the same no matter where they were. Whatever challenges I've had growing up would have been the same, I think, anywhere. We all have to work through issues passed along by our parents, and sooner or later we come to trust the redemptive power of God's grace in all situations.

Mary recalled that as children of missionaries, there were some incidents that turned out to be funny in hindsight.

When we left Liberia in 1963, my parents decided to do the 'grand tour' of the Middle East and Europe and take us to as many famous sites as possible. Of course we were traveling on a shoestring, but we went to Egypt, Israel, Lebanon, Italy, France, West Germany, Belgium, Switzerland, and England before finally returning to the United States. In Italy, we rented a car so we could drive around to different cities cheaply. On our last day in Italy, Dad and Charles went to return the car after dropping Mom and my sisters and me at the train station, where we would wait for them. We were running late (naturally). It was a massive place, like Grand Central Station. One of my sisters had to go to the bathroom so it became my job to take her while Mom waited for Dad and Charles. We found the bathroom all right but then got completely turned around and couldn't find Mom. No one around us spoke English. It was a scary situation! I don't recall whether I was praying but I'm sure someone, somewhere was praying for me. Eventually two Catholic nuns came up and helped us find the platform for the train to Paris, which was our next stop. Sure enough Mom was there waiting for us.

But where were my father and my brother? There were no cellphones back then, and the train was about to leave. Finally Mom just boarded the train in faith (they had the foresight to divide the tickets, so she had our tickets and Dad had the other two). The train pulled off. Eventually here came Dad and Charles walking down the aisle, looking for us. It was great to see them, and we all had a good laugh. "

FROM BETSY (Second Oldest daughter)
On one occasion, I had a little spending money and went to the store to buy candy. When I got home, Mom told me to offer the other kids some. Well, there happened to be a TON

of kids around, and I wasn't at all pleased with the prospect of having to share my candy with all of them. I had no problems envisioning my not having anything left for myself! But she stressed that we were to share what we had with others, no matter how little we had, or how badly we wanted it all for ourselves. So share I did.

Mom and Dad both moved slowly. And as they got older, although they both still participated in missions trips, the day got started more and more slowly when we were on the trips. Which means that we got finished with clinic later and later. One time in Haiti, there was rioting going on, and our driver was very concerned about leaving from a very dangerous part of Port-au-Price (Cite Soleil) to get back to the guesthouse before dark (which is when the rioting usually began). Well, Mom wasn't really interested in hearing what he had to say, and continued to move at her own pace. By the time we finished, it was pitch black, and our driver was just about beside himself. We ended up having to drive through part of the riots. Talk about praying….!

FROM CINDY (Widow of Oldest Son, Charles Jr.)
What t can I tell you about Mother Kennedy that isn't already known? She has been so many things to so many people, but perhaps as her daughter in law I may have experience a side

of her love that others haven't been blessed with. Although this may be hard, because I don't think she has ever met a person that she couldn't love with the help of her Savior. She's been involved with troubled inner city youth; involved with prison ministries, she's served on foreign fields, learning new languages and made daily sacrifices to learn about the people she was working with; she's lived with the prejudices and she loved every one with a love that can only come from a close relationship with her Lord and Savior, Jesus Christ.

Although she never aspired to being in politics she is well known and respected in the local political circles as one who fights for the needy people in our society, whether it be troubled students, troubled homeless individuals, people dealing with mental illness or people just simply hurting. She loves them – she loves them and they know it, even if they won't acknowledge it at first. And whether a person has millions of dollars or whether they are asking her for money, she treats them all the same – extending dignity, love and acceptance.

You often hear stories about one's mother in law. But I can honestly say I don't have any. Her love and concern for her family had always been evident. Charles and I spent two years in Mississippi and during that time she and Elder Kennedy came and visited with us. And I am sure if they had been able, they would've visited us when we were in Belize. Family was always important and she would let you know that you were special to her. Of course I only knew her from when I was an adult. But I do know that when she and Elder Kennedy went to Africa as missionaries, they already had two children (Charles and Mary) and when well-meaning church friends suggested that they not take the children with them, the response was that God knew they had children when He called them as missionaries and to Africa with them they went.

When Charles and I were married she sent me a letter stating that if I ever needed to talk about anything she was available. And she said if Charles and I ever had a problem she was willing to help us work things out. When Charles and I expressed an interest in doing mission work, she and Elder Kennedy came back from convocation and connected us with Bishop Bennett in Belize, where we served for two years. And when we then moved to Mississippi for two years, she prepared me for some of the southern customs (and prayed for us the entire time we were there, knowing some of the possible racial prejudices we might encounter).

She's a woman who gets thing done. She doesn't let worldly limitations stop her if she is convinced something should happen. She and Elder Kennedy founded Community Country Day School with probably no money at all – the school met in churches, received discarded books from the public school system, began with volunteer retired school teachers and staff and built up a campus that has provided an education to many who would not have otherwise been educated or become the productive citizens they are today.

Then she and Elder Kennedy founded two well-known homeless shelters in town – Community Shelter Services and Community of Caring. Both of these shelters provide much needed help in today's society. I believe she told me she had maybe $200 when she started community of caring and today it has an operating budget of around $370,000. If she believes God wants something done, she simply believes it will get done. Often if there were concerns about how payroll would be met, her response was usually "God will provide" And He did. I hope to one day be able to have my faith and trust be that strong, to not only be able to say He will provide but to totally believe it and to be able to have that be my first reaction to a situation.

Everywhere Mother has lived, people have been blessed. She still finds a way to get much needed funds to Africa and when any of the family are ill, we know that people are praying for us all over the world.

If you are around her very long you will hear her singing. She must have a song to help in any situation, whether it be a pleasant or sad time. She knows where her help is from (Jesus) and she knows the world to more songs than I could ever remember. Music has always been important in our family. During the hard time after Charles died, she would often share one with me that was especially helpful and that would help ease the pain and be able to press on. You can't sing God's praises and at the same time feel sorry for yourself. She's a living testimony of that.

I can honestly say that I have never heard her say a mean or vengeful statement about anyone – even though I know she has experienced reasons to express them. She doesn't dwell on negative things, but rather on how to make the world a better place and she instilled this message into her family – children, children's children and so on. The Kennedy legacy is a great one and she has done her very best to see that is continues.

FROM JENNIFER (Oldest grandchild)

Mother Marybeth Kennedy, also known as my grandmother, is quite a woman. I proudly claim rights as the first-born grandchild of her first-born son Charles. She has loved the Lord for twice as long as I have been alive! In public and in private she can often be found singing or humming old hymns or church songs. We all grew up loving music, in part probably due to her love of music. Not only is she a missionary and a visionary but she is also a poet. My grandfather loved singing as well – so singing was always a part of our lives. And their talents were continued on in the lives of their children – my father and aunt co-wrote quite a few songs.

Consistency is a key word I would use to describe my grandmother. Whether we were on the mission field together, worshipping together in church, or eating Sunday dinner, her attitude was the same – she didn't change personas once she went home. She is loving, caring, very intelligent, she loves to learn, she loves to laugh, and she intentionally enjoys life.

She is also very determined and very strong. Because of certain health conditions the doctors said she would be bed-ridden nearly two years ago, but by the grace of God (and sheer willpower) she is still walking! However, her every move brings pain. But yet she perseveres. Truly I don't think I could handle what she handles on a daily basis!

I have great memories: I remember her preparing to chase me around the table when I was little and called her granny instead of Grammy; memories of the times when we went grape-picking; or the trip to Africa with her and my grandfather when I was 13; the family reunion in Puerto Rico when they showed us the area where they had lived; or various trips to COGIC convocations; Easter dinners with her made-from-scratch pineapple upside down cake or her impromptu calling me to the microphone at an event to speak (we were supposed to always be prepared!); of family trips to the beach; of my college graduation where they actually showed up on time (it's a funny story); of her lovely purple dress worn at my wedding (a concession to my favorite color); or the kiss I gave her when I left her house last week.

As with everyone's personal story - our lives are a conglomeration of memories, of events, of people, of relationships, of how we walk out our personal salvation, of how we make it from day to day. We are more than just the person that people see on Sunday morning - we have history, we have feelings, we have personalities. No one is perfect, but isn't that the beauty of the life God gives us? God loved us enough to show us our flaws, gave us time to get the flaws corrected, and then turn back to Him. And then once we get ourselves right, our mission is to tell the world about God's love. Grammy has faithfully spread the message of God's love; she won't stop until God calls her home, and that's just alright with me.

FROM ANGELA (Daughter of Charles and Cindy who with her husband caries on legacy at Community Country Day School)

Growing up I always knew my grandparents were special. It was hard not to know that because everywhere we went we would hear that. They were instrumental in changing so many lives and establishing works that will live on. It wasn't until more recently that I began to fully appreciate and lean on my grandmother in a way I never had before.

My husband loved the school they started, Community Country Day School. It was started in 1969 for students that struggled to be accepted in a regular school setting. The school taught with love and is still doing this – the results are astounding!!! I never wanted to come back to work here but my husband felt led to leave his career in the CFL to come back and become the Executive Director. Approximately two years ago the financial situation at the school was getting hard. The school district wasn't paying their portion, donors were down and major funding sources were drying up. It was at this time my husband and I were able to see her extreme faith, strength and sheer resolve to not allow the dream to die. Even at the age of 86 she dug her heels in and coupled her prayers with action. She is a fund raiser like no other!! She knew how to ask even when it was EXTREMELY uncomfortable. I had heard her say that someone years prior had brought payroll to her door in a paper bag full of exactly the right amount of cash. My husband and I have learned so much from her through this time. Ministry is hard and exhausting at times. As a child I think I saw more of the life at home after you have spent yourself completely. Sometimes I would see them so tired there was not much else to give. I was always afraid of being just like her....so busy with ministry....what about my kids....I don't want to be used or attacked...well God has shown me through her that even when these times come, He is right there making you stronger than ever before. There were days I wanted to give up, the fear of not having enough money to keep the doors open was IMMENSE yet she did not waiver.

I remember during that time reading some of her poems she wrote and published in a book. Prior to this time I had seen the book and had a copy but never read it. During this time I started reading them and realized that each poem was written during hard times or happy times in her life. I began to draw strength knowing that my feelings were temporary but God would see us through just like he had for them. I am so thankful for the legacy my grandparents have left me. It is such a rare thing in this day. I have recently been able to go on trips with her to meet her friends and longtime ministry partners. It has been a sheer joy to watch her LIGHT up when she talks to the Saints. My family wants to be sure she isn't doing too much so she doesn't over extend. What I'm learning is that having purpose and living in it daily has given her a long life. She has a strong mind and still LOVES helping people as she is able. She is an example of someone pouring out their life and truly dying to self so that she may LIVE! I have recently been able to see not only the exhaustion that comes with giving your life away but the genuine excitement that can only come from obedience to God and following His plan for your life. I am so thankful for having a grandmother who is a hero, a scholar and most importantly a woman who followed God.

Aaron Collins (Angie's husband)
"Love Can Change the World"

Mother Mary Beth Kennedy is far more than pomp and circumstance. She is more than those with great ambition; more than those with the greatest intentions. She is love in action, love manifested. She is a living, breathing example of love and the power of love to change things, transform things, develop things. The power to make an indelible impact upon lives both local and worldwide.

Many talk about it, many dream about it. Mother Mary Beth Kennedy embodies it. She is a living example, a champion. She applies the ointment of God's love to those broken in this world. She is a star among stars. She is a leader of leaders. She stands alone as the trailblazer, leading us to believe and live lives yielded to God; available for God's all-consuming love to flow through us to the lovely souls of this world.

Other people have started schools, others are missionaries, others have opened shelters, and worked with orphans. They have done great works too. But I've not met one person who could not identify with the difference her agencies embody. The peace associated with her great work. She fosters the atmosphere of love.

God is love. God is welcome in all of the endeavors she has set out to do in His name. The power of His presence speaks to all that come into contact with these works. She is a true example of the power of a life surrendered to God. Mother Kennedy stands ALONE!!!

From Marva Cromartie Nyema, assists Mother Kennedy in her work in the DRC and spiritual daughter

Mother Kennedy to me is "Mother Theresa" in that she has impacted so many lives over these fifty years serving in so many countries. Despite her earned degrees, and being the top of her class, she is not too proud that she cannot mingle with the common people. She reminds me of a nun because of her head covering, and her white outfits she wears to churches and when she used to go to foreign countries.

Because of Elder & Mother Kennedy's experience in the foreign field, I was recommended to go to Haiti with them after being called to the foreign field as a full time missionary [to Liberia]. My first trip to Haiti was not too good for me [and] I left the team in Haiti. I was recommended to [first] go back to Haiti in the late 80's with the Kennedy's by the presiding mission board president Bishop Carlis Moody. During [this time], I learned how not to waste food. Discovering a "critter" being in my food, I wanted to get rid of it. Mother Kennedy shared with me how there were people who wished they had the beans and rice to eat and that I should eat around it. With the help of the Lord, I was able to do just that. This really was a learning experience for me.

Betty Gardner Harris (traveling companion), wrote this poem in honor of her mentor

COMMUNITY OF CARING

A place is provided for the poor and the needy,

It's called COC.

They come in all sizes, all ages all colors,

No prejudice there be

It's Mother Kennedy who God has chosen

Along with her family,

To begin this and take on the challenge here at COC

She won't have to worry when she goes to heaven,

The loves she shares has been free,

She is mentor and trainer,

So the work will continue

Through people like you and me

(From the book *Poems and Rhymes. . .*by Betty Gardner)

K

Nine

Honors, Awards, Creativeness and Resourcefulness

They have left their footprints in the lives of tens of thousands of individuals around the globe. They have also received numerous awards for their humanitarian efforts in the areas of social justice, education and philanthropy. Charles and Mary Beth were both awarded honorary doctorates in Public Service at Edisboro University in 1992. Mother Kennedy also received the United Way's Alexis de Tocqueville Award.

Throughout the interviews the recurring theme of each individual was that whatever situation the Kennedy's found themselves in, they trusted God to use the talents He bestowed upon them to accomplish His goal. Oldest daughter Mary said it best, "Mother taught us to take what you have to make what you want."

Erie Mayor Tullio presents a proclamation to CCDS

The Kennedys

Ever on the lookout for ways to generate needed funds for their ministry, the Kennedys brought back artifacts, paintings and other items from their travels to use at auctions. At one auction, proceeds exceeded $10,000!

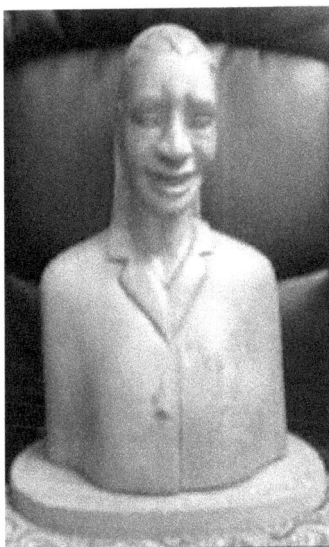

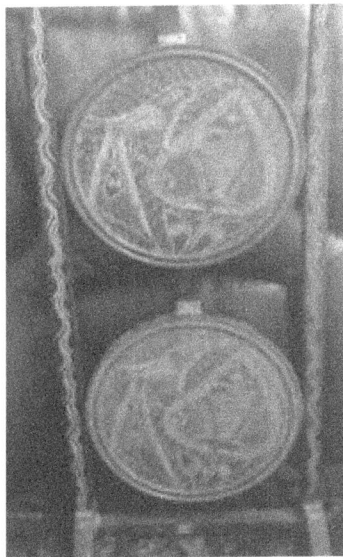

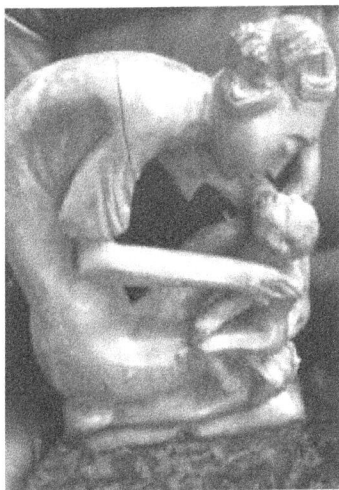

Guide to works of art given as personal gifts

1. Sign presented to Kennedys (Liberia)

2. Handmade busts of Dote, *"He stands alone"* and Kworo, *"she who conquers."* (DR Congo)

3. Wooden Drum *Back* (Liberia)

4. Wooden Drum *Front* (Liberia)

5. Oil painting of forest (DR Congo)

6. Handmade engraved stand

7. Mother and Child

8. The Thinker

9. Hand carved walking stick

10. Brass art object

11. Malachite period (DR Congo)

Father and Mother Kennedy have also been prolific writers with something to say! Her *Life in Wissikeh* written in 1958 provides a distinctive insight as she narrates the vicissitudes of everyday life on the mission field. Currently books are sold to undergird some of the expenses for Community of Caring and other ministry efforts.

Below are excerpts from her book of poetry *The Love of God*

Commitment

THE CROSS

I wear the sign of Your cross,
But am I willing to bear
That cross when it means disappointment
Or trouble or deep despair?

And when Your cross means sickness,
Painful and dreary and long,
When my moments are measured in misery
And You've taken away my song?

Or when it means great darkness,
When all that is good seems lost,
When my mind's filled with trouble and sorrow,
Am I willing to carry that cross?
I mark my home with Your cross,
Lord, let it be more than a sign,
Let me willingly shoulder my burden,
Let me know that each cross is divine.

TRIBUTE TO ELDER CHARLES KENNEDY, SR.

In faith he went to stop a war

Wild animals assailed

And even fiercer men, but still

God's mighty power prevailed.

And once the jeep climbed up a hill,

Carrying a heavy load.

It started to slip

And the wheels left the ground,

Angels pushed those wheels back on the road.

Once we reached a mighty river

Where there was no ferry boat,

He built a raft of bamboo and barrels,

And declared that thing would float!

He drove the jeep and that fragile bark

Its worthiness displayed,

He crossed the river with our only son,

While I stood on the bank and prayed!

Long years ago he promised God

His love and devotion would never cease.

He kept his word and we honor him,

Man of courage. . .man of peace!

Father Kennedy's wrote on a variety of subjects. He thoroughly embraced the integration of science and theology and the power of his argument impressed most who reflected upon it. Following is an excerpt from one paper written by Father Kennedy.

There is a widespread misunderstanding about science, namely that science is limited to the study of matter. Actually science can deal with any subject that can be observed. It is a method of study that can be summarized in three words: observation, verification, explanation. We observe facts, verify them and try to get meaning from them, to discover relations between the facts. There is one aspect of this that is not often mentioned. Any one of us approaches a problem with a certain set of data and assumptions, or even a philosophy...This affects how we use the scientific methods and what we apply it to. In high school, some experienced this in Euclidean geometry. We had no reason to question those postulates. In fact hardly anyone questioned them for a couple thousand years. But in the last century Einstein and others have questioned...and soon there were other geometries...and they have meaning.

Something like this has happened in science. I would venture to say that some of the (unwritten) postulates for "natural" science are:

1. We will limit ourselves to the study of inert matter.
2. Inert matter exists in time and space.
3. The fundamental dimensions for our study are three: time, distance and matter.

4. We do study living things, but life does not exist apart from matter.

5. If there are any other things, such as life, love, soul, spirit, God, right and wrong, those are not included in our science, but in subjects such as religion and philosophy.

Now some of us who believe the Bible are questioning these postulates. They are perfectly good for natural science, but there are too limiting for a general science...People are postulating that there is such a thing as an intelligent designer. That is because the chances for matter by itself to behave in such as manner as to create life are so astronomically low as to be impossible.

It is good science to choose postulates, as the naturalists have done. It is better science to name the postulates. It is also good science for us to choose our postulates. The idea is to choose postulates that agree with the Bible and that we already have reason to believe they are true. Then we try them and see if we can build a science around them that will fit the things we observe. What that amounts to is considering the Bible scientifically. That is, if we took it just on faith, that would be pure religion. Some of us don't believe until we see. But we have seen enough of the Bible truths work out in our own experience that now we believe. That is the verifying part of science, and that's what make sour study scientific. *Elder Charles Kennedy Sr. Erie Times News*

Some Final Thoughts

There has never been any considerable competition for venturing out into the international mission field. In the public consciousness today, missions work is for that otherworldly, serious or no nonsense person satisfied to live a sad life of lack and despair. The happy confluence of events that caused the Kennedy's to meet was no coincidence. It had its genesis in a divine imperative causing the profile to be debunked. This is not to say that those who chose not to enter foreign services are without peace or joy. The postulate is that whatever the plan of God, in order to be content in one's productivity, the individual purpose must align. The scholarly yet humorous Charles and his witty and effervescent wife Mary Beth championed that idea, yes there was suffering or times of lack, *but they did not have to!* Contrary to a life suited to their intellectual prowess and educational accomplishments, they chose to seal their fate by saying yes to God's will. Despite setbacks this demonstration of faith caused them to experience the undergirding of joy that they were faithful to the assignment God tasked them with. Because they did not hide their talents in the grounds of affluence, this great man and woman, exemplars of the faith, could indeed reflect that for them *It's Been A Good Life!*

If you like this book you may also be interested in the following books and DVDs from HCM Publishing by Glenda Williams Goodson

I Want My Life to Reach Out and Touch Somebody!
A BIOGRAPHY: Gladys Venolia Johnny Ray Alexander
Williams, Church Planter (2014)

ROYALTY UNVEILED: *Women Trailblazers in Church Of God
In Christ International Missions
1920 – 1970*
(2011)

**I'm So Glad I'm Sanctified: Wisdom Quotes and Treasures
from COGIC Pioneering Women
1911-1975** (2005)

Bishop Mason and Those Sanctified Women!
(2004)

**Our Mothers' Stories: History of the Department of Women
with live interviews from COGIC pioneers**
80 minute documentary on DVD (2004)

Other HCM Authors
Toll Free: Scriptural Insight, Inspiration and Devotionals for
Everyday by Pearl White (2012)

728 Sewell Dr.
Lancaster, Texas 75146
glendagoodson@aol.com

~~

To contact Community of Caring
245 East 8th Street Erie, PA 16503
(814) 456-6661

www.ingramcontent.com/pod-product-compliance
Lightning Source LLC
Chambersburg PA
CBHW060433090426
42733CB00011B/2263